# SMALL CRAFT WARNINGS

# By TENNESSEE WILLIAMS

### PLAYS

Baby Doll (a screenplay)
Camino Real
Cat on a Hot Tin Roof
Dragon Country
The Glass Menagerie
A Lovely Sunday for Creve Coeur
Small Craft Warnings
A Streetcar Named Desire
Sweet Bird of Youth
THE THEATRE OF TENNESSEE WILLIAMS, VOLUME I
  *Battle of Angels, A Streetcar Named Desire, The Glass Menagerie*
THE THEATRE OF TENNESSEE WILLIAMS, VOLUME II
  *The Eccentricities of a Nightingale, Summer and Smoke, The Rose Tattoo, Camino Real*
THE THEATRE OF TENNESSEE WILLIAMS, VOLUME III
  *Cat on a Hot Tin Roof, Orpheus Descending, Suddenly Last Summer*
THE THEATRE OF TENNESSEE WILLIAMS, VOLUME IV
  *Sweet Bird of Youth, Period of Adjustment, The Night of the Iguana*
THE THEATRE OF TENNESSEE WILLIAMS, VOLUME V
  *The Milk Train Doesn't Stop Here Anymore, Kingdom of Earth (The Seven Descents of Myrtle), Small Craft Warnings, The Two-Character Play*
THE THEATRE OF TENNESSEE WILLIAMS, VOLUME VI
  *27 Wagons Full of Cotton and Other Short Plays*
THE THEATRE OF TENNESSEE WILLIAMS, VOLUME VII
  *In the Bar of a Tokyo Hotel and Other Plays*
27 Wagons Full of Cotton and Other Plays
The Two-Character Play
Vieux Carré

### POETRY

Androgyne, Mon Amour
In the Winter of Cities

### PROSE

Eight Mortal Ladies Possessed
Hard Candy and Other Stories
The Knightly Quest and Other Stories
One Arm and Other Stories
The Roman Spring of Mrs. Stone
Where I Live: Selected Essays

# SMALL CRAFT WARNINGS

by TENNESSEE WILLIAMS

A NEW DIRECTIONS BOOK

Manufactured in the United States of America

Published simultaneously in Canada by McClelland & Stewart, Ltd.

First published clothbound (ISBN: 0-8112-0460-x) and as
New Directions Paperbook 348 (ISBN: 0-8112-0461-8) in 1972.

New Directions Books are published for James Laughlin
by New Directions Publishing Corporation,
80 Eighth Avenue, New York 10011

FIFTH PRINTING

# SMALL CRAFT WARNINGS

# TOO PERSONAL?*

The greatest danger, professionally, of becoming the subject of so many "write-ups" and personal appearances on TV and lecture platforms is that the materials of your life, which are, in the case of all organic writing, the materials of your work, are sort of telegraphed in to those who see you and to those who read about you. So, when you get to the serious organization of this material into your work, people (meaning audiences and critics—all but the few most tolerant whom you naturally regard as the best) have a sort of *déjà vu* or *déjà entendu* reaction to these materials which you have submitted to the cathartic process of your "sullen craft and art."

You may justifiably wonder why a man of my years in his profession, recognizing this hazard, has yet been willing to expose himself (with a frequency which seems almost symptomatic of clinical exhibitionism) to all of these interviews and the fewer, but equally personal, exposures on platform and "the tube."

I can offer you at least two reasons for this phenomenon. One is probably something with which you will immediately empathize. When one has passed through an extensive period of that excess of privacy which is imposed upon a person drifting almost willfullly out of contact with the world, anticipating that final seclusion of the nonbeing, there comes upon him, when that period wears itself out and he is still alive, an almost insatiable hunger for recognition of the fact that he is, indeed, still alive, both as man and artist. That's reason number one. The other is rather comical, I'm afraid. You get a devastatingly

* This was meant to be submitted to *The New York Times* as a preopening piece, but they chose to interview me instead.—T. W.

**3**

bad write-up, and you feel that you are washed up for good. Then some magazine editor gets through to you on that phone in the studio of your tropical retreat, the phone that you never pick up till it's rung so persistently that you assume that your secretary and house guests have been immobilized by nerve gas or something of that nature, and this editor speaks to you as sympathetically as the family doctor to a child stricken with a perforated appendix and tells you that he is as shocked as you were by the tasteless exposé-type of interview which appeared about you in a recent issue of some other mag. And then, of course, you forget about work, and you rage yourself into a slather over the iniquities and duplicities of the "interviewer" referred to. You say, "Why, that creature was so drunk he didn't know what street I lived on, and the guy that set me up for him laced my martini with sodium penathol, and all I remember about this occasion is that my head came off my shoulders and hit the ceiling and I heard myself babbling away like an hysteric and I hadn't the slightest notion that he had a concealed tape recorder with him, and later he offered to play bridge with me that night, and he came over again with the tape recorder in some orifice of his body, I presume, and you know I do not see well and you know I like to hold forth to apparently amiable listeners, and I just assume that when they say 'I am interested only in your work,' that that's what they mean."

Now the editor has you on the hook.

"That's exactly my reaction to the revolting piece and how about letting us do a piece to correct it?"

You grasp at this offer like a drowning rat climbs on to anything that will float it. So you get another write-up. Then after this write-up, which is usually more colorful and better written than the one before, but equally nonserious, if not downright clownish, you feel that it is a life-or-death matter, professionally, with a new play opening somewhere, to correct the hilarious misquotes and exaggerations which embellished the second write-up, and so you go on to others and others. Now at last you have poured out, compulsively and perhaps fatally, all the recent content of your experience which should have been held in reserve for its proper place, which is in the work you're doing every morning (which, in my case, is the writing I do every morning).

Is it or is it not right or wrong for a playwright to put his persona into his work?

My answer is: "What else can he do?"—I mean the very root-necessity of all creative work is to express those things most involved in his experience. Otherwise, is the work, however well executed, not a manufactured, a synthetic thing? I've said, perhaps repeatedly, that I have two major classifications for writing: that which is organic and that which is not. And this opinion still holds.

Now let me attempt to entertain you once more with an anecdote.

Long ago, in the early forties, I attended a very posh party given by the Theatre Guild. I was comfortably and happily seated at a small table with my dear friend Miss Jo Healy, who was receptionist at the Guild in those days, when a lady with eyes that blazed with some nameless frenzy rushed up to me like a guided missile and seized me by the arm and shrieked to me, "You've got to meet Miss Ferber, she's dying to meet you."

Now in those days I was at least pliable, and so I permitted myself to be hauled over to a large table at which were seated a number of Diamond T trucks disguised as ladies.

"Oh, Miss Ferber," shrieked my unknown pilot, "this is Tennessee Williams."

Miss Ferber gazed slowly up and delivered this annihilating one-liner:

"The best I can manage is a mild 'Yippee.'"

"Madam," I said, "I can't even manage that."

Now everyone knows, who is cognizant of the world of letters, that Miss Edna Ferber was a creature of mammoth productivity and success. She was good at doing her thing; her novel and picture sales are fairly astronomical, I would guess.

I bring her up because she represents to me the classic, the archetypal, example of a writer whose work is impersonal, at least upon any recognizable level. I cannot see her in the oil fields of Texas with Rock Hudson and the late James Dean. Nor can I see her in any of her other impressive epics. I see her only as a lady who chose to put down a writer who was then young and vulnerable with such a gratuitously malicious one-liner. I mean without provocation, since I had literally been dragged to the steps of her throne.

So far I have spoken only in defense of the personal kind of writing. Now I assure you that I know it can be overdone. It is the responsibility of the writer to put his experience as a being into work that refines it and elevates it and that makes of it an essence that a wide audience can somehow manage to feel in themselves: "This is true."

In all human experience, there are parallels which permit common understanding in the telling and hearing, and it is the frightening responsibility of an artist to make what is directly or allusively close to his own being communicable and under-standable, however disturbingly, to the hearts and minds of all whom he addresses.

T.W.
March 26, 1972

**6**

*Small Craft Warnings* was presented at the Truck and Warehouse Theatre in New York on April 2, 1972, by Ecco Productions, Robert Currie, Mario De Maria, William Orton. It was directed by Richard Altman; the stage setting and costumes were by Fred Voelpel, lighting by John Gleason; production stage manager, Robert Currie. The cast was as follows:

| | |
|---|---|
| VIOLET | CHERRY DAVIS |
| DOC | DAVID HOOKS |
| MONK | GENE FANNING |
| BILL McCORKLE | BRAD SULLIVAN |
| LEONA DAWSON | HELENA CARROLL |
| STEVE | WILLIAM HICKEY |
| QUENTIN | ALAN MIXON |
| BOBBY | DAVID HUFFMAN |
| TONY, THE COP | JOHN DAVID KEES |

SKETCH OF STAGE SETTING FOR THE NEW YORK PRODUCTION, BY JOHN WENGER

Act I: A bar along the Southern California Coast

Act II: An hour or two later

*The curtain rises. The sound of ocean wind is heard. The stage is lighted at a very low level.*

*The scene is a somewhat nonrealistic evocation of a bar on the beach-front in one of those coastal towns between Los Angeles and San Diego. It attracts a group of regular patrons who are nearly all so well known to each other that it is like a community club, and most of these regulars spend the whole evening there. Ideally, the walls of the bar, on all three sides, should have the effect of fog rolling in from the ocean. A blue neon outside the door says: "Monk's Place." The bar runs diagonally from upstage to down; over it is suspended a large varnished sailfish, whose gaping bill and goggle-eyes give it a constant look of amazement. There are about three tables, with red-checked tablecloths. Stage right there is a juke box, and in the wall at right are doors to the ladies' and gents' lavatories. A flight of stairs ascends to the bar-owner's living quarters. The stairs should be masked above the first few steps.*

*The bar interior is dimly, evenly lit at rise. At some time in the course of the play, when a character disengages himself from the group to speak as if to himself, the light in the bar should dim, and a special spot should illuminate each actor as he speaks.*

*Monk is behind the bar serving Doc. Monk, the bar-owner, and Doc, who lost his license for heavy drinking but still practices more or less clandestinely, are middle-aged.*

*At a downstage table sits Violet, at her feet a battered suitcase fastened with a rope. Her eyes are too large for her face, and they are usually moist: her appearance suggests a derelict kind of existence; still, she has about her a pale, bizarre sort of beauty. As Leona Dawson later puts it, she's like a water plant.*

MONK [*to Doc*]: Notice? [*He nods his head.*] Over there?

[*Doc emerges from introspection to glance the way indicated by Monk. They both gaze at Violet.*]

VIOLET [*singing a bit, self-conscious under their scrutiny*]:
The wheel of fortune
Keeps turning around . . .
[*She can't remember past this.*]

DOC [*voice filtered through booze*]: Oh, yes, she's a noticeable thing. She has a sort of not-quite-with-it appearance. Amorphous, that's the word. Something more like a possibility than a completed creature.

MONK: What I mean is the *suitcase. With* her.

DOC: Oh, yes, the suitcase. Does she think she's in the waiting room of a depot?

MONK: I think she thinks she's moved in here.

DOC: Oh. That's a possible problem for you there.

MONK: You're Goddam right. I'm running a tavern that's licensed to dispense spirits, not a pad for vagrants. You see, they see those stairs. They know I live up there.

DOC: Yep, they see those stairs to the living quarters above, and it hits them dimly that you might need the solace of their companionship up there some nights when they find it convenient to offer it to you, and I don't need to tell you that this solace of companionship is not the least expensive item on the shelves of the fucking supermarket a man of my age has to spend what's left of his life in. Oh, that solace, that comfort of companionship is on the shelves of the market even for me, but I tell you, the price is inflated on it. I had me one last summer. Remember that plump little Chicano woman used to come in here with me some nights last summer? A little wet-leg woman, nice boobs on her and a national monument for an ass? Well, she came to me for medical attention.

[*Monk laughs heartily at this.*

[*Bill enters the bar; he comes up to it with an overrelaxed amiability like a loser putting up a bold front: by definition, a "stud"—but what are definitions?*

[*Monk mechanically produces Bill's can of Miller's but doesn't open it for him.*]

She had worms, diet of rotten beef tacos, I reckon, or tamales or something. I diagnosed it correctly. I gave her the little bottle and the wooden spoon and I said to her, "Bring me in a sample of your stool for lab analysis." She didn't know what I meant. Language barrier. I finally said, "Señorita, bring a little piece of your shit in the bottle tomorrow." [*He and Monk laugh heartily.*]

[*Bill is worried over the fact his beer can is not opened and served.*]

VIOLET: Hey, Bill . . .

DOC: Some beginning of some romance. Dewormed the lady and laid her in place of payment. Jesus, what a love story. I had her all summer, but in September she met a good-looking young pimp who made her critical of me. She called me a dirty old man, so I let her go.

BILL: Hey, Monk. About that beer.

MONK [*ignoring Bill*]: I don't remember you coming in here with a woman.

DOC: We always sat at a back table arguing over the fair expense of her ass.

BILL: Jesus, Monk, how big a tab has Leona run up here!? For Chrissake! [*He leans across the bar and snatches the can of*

*Miller's from Monk's hand. Monk had ignored him only half deliberately and is annoyed by the grab.*]

MONK: Look, I don't run Leona's tab through a computer, since I know she's good for it. If you want the can opened, give it back here. [*He opens the can.*] Now if it was your tab, not hers, I'd worry, but since it's hers, not yours, I don't. OK? No offense, no complaint, just . . .

VIOLET: Bill?

BILL: I could tell you some things.

MONK: Why don't you tell 'em to Violet, she's called you three times.

BILL [*glancing at her*]: Hi, Vi.

VIOLET: I had an awful experience today with Mr. Menzies at the amusement arcade. [*Sobbing sound*] Oh, I don't know what to do. Min broke in. Last night. Menzies said I . . . Come over here so I can tell you. Oh, and bring me a beer and a pepperoni, I'm famished. Lonesome and famished.

BILL: You want me to solve both those situations for you?

VIOLET: Yes, please.

BILL [*to Monk*]: Another Miller's and a coupla Slim Jims.

MONK: Yep, I got that message. Have you left Leona?

VIOLET: Bill, where's Leona?

BILL: Crying into a stew in her Goddam trailer.

[*Monk opens another beer, and Bill ambles over to Violet with the pepperonis and beer and the smile he meets the world with. It is a hustler's smile, the smile of a professional stud— now aging a bit but still with considerable memorabilia of his young charm.*]

VIOLET: Thanks, Bill . . .

[*Monk is toying with a radio which is over the bar.*]

RADIO VOICE: Heavy seas from Point Conception south to the Mexican border, fog continuing till tomorrow noon, extreme caution should be observed on all highways along this section of the coastline.

MONK [*ironically, turning off radio*]: Small craft warnings, Doc.

DOC: That's right, Monk, and you're running a place of refuge for vulnerable human vessels, and . . .

VIOLET: [*closer to Bill*]: Have you left Leona? For good?

BILL: Just till she gets her knickers out of that twist. She had this brother, a faggot that played the fiddle in church, and whenever she's drunk, she starts to cry up a storm about this little fag that she admitted was arrested for loitering in the Greyhound bus station men's room, and if I say, "Well, he was asking for it," she throws something at me.

VIOLET [*leaning amorously toward him*]: A man like you.

BILL: A man like me?

VIOLET: A bull of a man like you. You got arms on you big as the sides of a ham. [*She strokes his bare arm.*]

BILL: That ain't all I got big.

VIOLET: You mean what I think?

BILL: If you can't see you can feel.

[*She reaches under the table, and it is obvious that she is feeling him.*]

A man likes appreciation. Now I got a letter this week from a female guv'ment employee in Sacramento who's a Reagan supporter.

**15**

VIOLET: Huh?

BILL: Shit. She ain't seen me since '65 but remembers me clearly and wants me back on her aquabed with her, and if you've slept in an aquabed it don't matter who's in it with you.

[*The door bursts open. Leona enters like a small bull making his charge into the ring. Leona, a large, ungainly woman, is wearing white clam-digger slacks and a woolly pink sweater. On her head of dyed corkscrew curls is a sailor's hat which she occasionally whips off her head to slap something with— the bar, a tabletop, somebody's back—to emphasize a point. There are abrupt changes of position at the downstage table at her entrance, but she notices only Bill there.*]

LEONA: YOUUUUU . . . MOTHER! I was talkin' to you from the stove and you weren't there!

[*Bill chuckles and winks.*]

Three hours I spent shopping for and preparing a . . . memorial dinner while you watched TV.

BILL: Stew and veg.

LEONA [*lyrically, as a pop-poem*]: Lamb stew with garden fresh vegetables from the Farmer's Market, seasoned with bay leaves, and rosemary and thyme.

BILL: Stew.

LEONA: I'd set up a little banquet table in that trailer tonight, my grandmother's silver and Irish lace tablecloth, my crystal candlesticks with the vine leaves filigreed on 'em in silver which I'd polished, all spit-polished for this memorial dinner, set the candles on either side of my single rose vase containing a single talisman rose just opened, a table like a photo from *House and Garden*. I talk from the stove to no one. I open the fridge to get out the jellied bouillon, madrilene, topped with . . . "Okayyyy,

**16**

ready." I come in and I'm received by the TV set and the trailer door hanging open, and in the confusion I knock over and break my cut-glass decanter of Burgundy, imported.

BILL: I went out for a bottle. You'd kilt a fifth of Imp. She was crying in the stew to save on salt.

LEONA: Without word or a note on the table. You went! Why? For what?

VIOLET: Leona, Bill's not happy tonight, so let him be.

LEONA: Two people's not happy and one of 'em with *reason!* Is that your suitcase with you? Are you thrown out, evicted? A lady of the street? Oh, my God, here's a good one I heard at the shop today about a pair of street-ladies in Dublin. One enters a pub, elegant but pissed, and she says to the barman, "Two gins for two ladies." He observes her condition and says, "Where is the other lady?" "The other lady," she says, "is in the gutter, resting." [*Only she is amused by the story.*] Oh, well, I thought it was funny. [*Leona sits at table with Violet and Bill.*] Violet, dear, will you look at your nails?

VIOLET: I know, the enamel's chipping.

LEONA: Yes! Exposing the dirt.

[*Violet drops her hands under the table.*]

Oh, my God, forget it, forget the whole enchilada. Not worth a thought.

[*No response.*]

Excuse me a moment. I'm going to press one button three times on that multiselector, and Violet, here's an orange stick for your nails . . . Don't be depressed. A sure cure for depression is the ax.

VIOLET: I'm not depressed.

LEONA [*laughing*]: Then you must not be conscious. [*She crosses to the juke box.*] I hope nobody objects to the number

**17**

I play. It's going to be played here repeatedly tonight, appreciated or not. [*She bends over the juke box to find the desired number, which she herself contributed to the "Classicals" on the box.*] Róck? No! Popular? No! Classicals—yes! Number? Number? Which?

VIOLET: Tell her I'm not depressed.

[*Violet's hand has dropped under the table. It is apparent that she is reaching for Bill.*]

BILL: *She's* depressed . . . and depressing. [*Leans back luxuriously in chair. A look to Leona. He speaks with emphasis, rather than volume.*] . . . Not bad, huh? A definite . . . personal . . . asset?

[*Monk turns up radio. Gets static.*]

LEONA: Do you have to turn that on when I'm . . .

[*At this precise moment she is caught by the change in attitudes at the downstage table. Her eyes widen; her hands clench; she takes a couple of paces toward the table and crouches a bit to peer under it. Then quick as a shot:*]

YOUUU . . . CUNT!

[*She charges.*

[*Violet screams and springs up, overturning her chair.*]

MONK: Hold her!

[*Bill's massive frame obstructs Leona, not only her motion but her view of Violet. Bill is holding her by both shoulders, grinning into her face.*

[*The following lines overlap.*]

LEONA: OFF HANDS!

MONK: Nope, nope, nope, nope, nope!

LEONA: McCorkle, DON' YOU ...!

MONK: Keep her at that table!

[*During this Monk has crossed from behind the bar.*

[*Violet has turned about dizzily, then fled into the ladies'.*

[*Leona stamps on Bill's foot. He yells, falls back an instant, releasing her. As she rushes forward, he gives her a hard slap on the butt; she turns to give him battle, and is caught from behind by Monk. She kicks at Monk's shin, and gives Bill a wallop in the face with her cap.*]

BILL [*rubbing his eyes*]: Goddam, she ...

MONK: I'm havin' no violence here! Never! None! From no one!

[*A sudden hush falls: a sudden moment of stillness in a corrida.*]

LEONA [*incredulously, profoundly, hurtly, right into Bill's face*]: YOU! Let *her!* In front of ME? ... in PUBLIC! ... In a BAR!

BILL: What the fuck of it! You hit me right in the eyes with ...

LEONA [*makes a big-theater turn and shouts*]: Where *IS* she? Where's she gone? [*Receiving no answer—there is still no sound from Violet's place of refuge—she suddenly rushes for the stairs.*]

MONK: Nobody's up my stairs! Come down those ...

[*Violet's lamentation begins.*]

LEONA: Aw! She's gone to the LADIES'! Change the name on that door.

MONK: I'm operating a place for gents and ladies. [*He is panting a bit.*]

**19**

LEONA: Gents and . . . what?

MONK: Ladies.

LEONA: Aw, now, Monk. I thought you run a clean place but don't come on with . . . her? Lady? Him? Gent? [*She points toward the ladies' room and then toward Bill.*] There's limits to . . .

MONK: Yes. Stay away from . . .

[*Leona had started toward the ladies'. Monk blocks her. She throws her head back and utters an apocalyptic outcry. It's like the outcry of all human protest.*]

No more disturbance of . . .

LEONA [*drawing herself up heroically as she confronts Monk almost nose-to-nose*]: LET ME SET YOU STRAIGHT ABOUT WHAT'S A LADY! A lady's a woman, with respect for herself and for relations of others! HER? IN THERE? WAILING? RESPECT FOR? . . . She's got no respect for herself and that is the single respect in which she's correct to! No one could blame her for that! [*She has resumed her pacing and slapping at things with sailor's cap.*] What could she possibly find to respect in herself? She lives like an animal in a room with no bath that's directly over the amusement arcade at the foot of the pier, yeah, right over the billiards, the pinball games, and the bowling alleys at the amusement arcade, it's bang, bang, bang, loud as a TV western all day and all night, and then bang, bang again at eight A.M. It would drive a sane person crazy but she couldn't care less. She don't have a closet, she didn't have a bureau so she hangs her dresses on a piece of rope that hangs across a corner between two nails, and her other possessions she keeps on the floor in boxes.

BILL: What business is it of yours?

LEONA: None, not a Goddam bit! When she was sick? I went there to bring her a chicken. I asked her, where is your silver?

She didn't have any silver, not a fork, spoon, or knife, hell, not even a plate, but she ate the chicken, aw, yeah, she ate the chicken like a dog would eat it, she picked it up in her paws and gnawed at it just like a dog. Who came to see if she was living or dead? ME! ONLY! I got her a bureau, I got her a knife, fork, and spoon, I got her china, I got her a change of bed linen for her broken-down cot, and ev'ry day after work I come by that Goddam rathole with a bottle of hot beef bouillon or a chicken or meatloaf to see what she needed and bring it, and then one time I come by there to see what she needed and bring it. The bitch wasn't there. I thought my God she's died or they put her away. I run downstairs, and I heard her screaming with joy in the amusement arcade. She was having herself a ball with a shipload of drunk sailor boys; she hardly had time to speak to me.

BILL: Maybe she'd gotten sick of you. That's a possible reason.

LEONA: It's a possible reason I was sick of her, too, but I'd thought that the bitch was dying of malnutrition, and I thought she was human, and a human life is worth saving or what the shit *is* worth saving. But is she human? She's just a parasite creature, not even made out of flesh but out of wet biscuit dough, she always looks like the bones are dissolving in her.

BILL [*banging his beer bottle on the table*]: DO YOU THINK I BELONG TO YOU? I BELONG TO MYSELF, I JUST BELONG TO MYSELF.

LEONA: Aw, you pitiful piece of . . . worthless . . . conceit! [*She addresses the bar.*] . . . Never done a lick of work in his life . . . He has a name for his thing. He calls it Junior. He says he takes care of Junior and Junior takes care of him. How long is that gonna last? How long does he figure Junior is going to continue to provide for him, huh? HUH! . . . Forever or *less* than forever? . . . Thinks the sun rises and sets between his legs and that's the reason I put him in my trailer, feed him, give him

**21**

beer-money, pretend I don't notice there's five or ten bucks less in my pocketbook in the morning than my pocketbook had in it when I fell to sleep, night before.

BILL: Go out on the beach and tell that to the sea gulls, they'd be more int'rested in it.

VIOLET [*shrilly, from the ladies' room*]: Help me, help me, somebody, somebody call the po-liiiiice!

LEONA: Is she howling out the ladies' room window?

VIOLET: How long do I have to stay in here before you get the police?

LEONA: If that fink is howling out the ladies' room window, I'm going out back and throw a brick in at her.

MONK: Leona, now cool it, Leona.

LEONA: I'll pay the damage, I'll pay the hospital expenses.

MONK: Leona, why don't you play your violin number on the box and settle down at a table and . . .

LEONA: When I been insulted by someone, I don't settle down at a table, or nowhere, NOWHERE!

[*Violet sobs and wails as Steve comes into the bar. Steve is wearing a floral-patterned sports shirt under a tan jacket and the greasy white trousers of a short-order cook.*]

STEVE: Is that Violet in there?

LEONA: Who else do you think would be howling out the ladies' room window but her, and you better keep out of this, this is between her and me.

STEVE: What happened? Did you hit Violet?

LEONA: You're Goddam right I busted that filthy bitch in the kisser, and when she comes out of the ladies', if she ever comes out, I'm gonna bust her in the kisser again, and kiss my ass, I'm just the one that can do it! MONK! DRINK! BOURBON SWEET!

MONK: Leona, you're on a mean drunk, and I don't serve liquor to no one on a mean drunk.

LEONA: Well, you can kiss it, too, you monkey-faced mother. [*She slaps the bar top with her sailor hat.*]

STEVE: Hey, did you hit Violet?

[*Bill laughs at this anticlimactic question.*]

LEONA: Have you gone deaf, have you got wax in your ears, can't you hear her howling in there? Did I hit Violet? The answer is yes, and I'm not through with her yet. [*Leona approaches the door of the ladies' room.*] COME ON OUT OF THERE, VIOLET, OR I'LL BREAK IN THE DOOR! [*She bangs her fist on the door, then slaps it contemptuously with her cap, and resumes her pacing.*]

[*Bill keeps grinning and chuckling.*]

STEVE: Why did she hit Violet?

LEONA: Why don't you ask *me* why?

STEVE: Why did you hit Violet?

LEONA: I hit Violet because she acted indecent with that son of a bitch I been supporting for six months in my trailer.

STEVE: What do you mean "indecent"?

LEONA: Jesus, don't you know her habits? Are you unconscious ev'ry night in this bar and in her rathole over the amusement arcade? I mean she acted indecent with her dirty paws under the table. I came in here tonight and saw her hands on the table. The red enamel had nearly all chipped off the nails and the fingernails, black, I mean *black*, like she'd spend every day for

**23**

a month without washing her hands after making mud-pies with filthy motherless kids, and I thought to myself, it's awful, the degradation a woman can sink down into without respect for herself, so I said to her, Violet, will you look at your hands, will you look at your fingernails, Violet?

STEVE: Is that why you hit Violet?

LEONA: Goddam it, NO! Will you listen? I told her to look at her nails and she said, oh, the enamel is peeling, I know. I mean the dirtiness of the nails was not a thing she could notice, just the chipped red enamel.

STEVE: Is that why you hit Violet?

LEONA: Shit, will you shut up till I tell you why I hit her? I wouldn't hit her just for being unclean, unsanitary. I wouldn't hit her for nothing that affected just her. And now, if you'll pay attention, I'm going to tell you exactly why I did hit her. I got up from the table to play "Souvenir."

STEVE: What is she talking about? What are you talking about?

LEONA: When I come back to the table her hands had disappeared off it. I thought to myself, I'm sorry, I made her ashamed of her hands and she's hiding them now.

STEVE: Is that why you hit Violet?

LEONA: Why do you come in a bar when you're already drunk? No! Listen! It wasn't embarrassment over her filthy nails that had made her take her hands off the table top, it was her old habit, as filthy as her nails. The reason her pitiful hands had disappeared off the table was because under the table she was acting indecent with her hands in the lap of that ape that moved himself into my trailer and tonight will move himself out as fast as he moved himself in. And now do you know why

I hit her? If you had balls, which it doesn't look like you do, you would've hit her yourself instead of making me do it.

STEVE: I wasn't there when it happened, but that's the reason you hit her?

LEONA: Yeah, now the reason has got through the fog in your head, which is thick as the fog on the beach.

[*Violet wails from the ladies' room.*]

STEVE: I'm not married to Violet, I never was or will be. I just wanted to know who hit her and why you hit her.

LEONA [*slapping at him with her cap*]: Annhh!

STEVE: Don't slap at me with that cap. What do I have to do with what she done or she does?

LEONA: No responsibility? No affection? No pity? You stand there hearing her wailing in the ladies' and deny there's any connection between you? Well, now I feel sorry for her. I regret that I hit her. She can come back out now and I won't hit her again. I see her life, the awfulness of her hands reaching out under a table, automatically creeping under a table into the lap of anything with a thing that she can catch hold of. Let her out of the ladies', I'll never hit her again. I feel too much pity for her, but I'm going out for a minute to breathe some clean air and to get me a drink where a barman's willing to serve me, and then I'll come back to pay up whatever I owe here and say good-bye to the sailfish, hooked and shellacked and strung up like a flag over . . . over . . . lesser, much lesser . . . creatures that never, ever sailed an inch in their . . . lives . . .

[*The pauses at the end of this speech are due to a shift of her attention toward a young man and a boy who have entered the bar. Her eyes have followed them as they walked past her to a table in the front.*]

[*She continues speaking, but now as if to herself.*]

. . . When I leave here tonight, none of you will ever see me again. I'm going to stop by the shop, let myself in with my passkey and collect my own equipment, which is enough to open a shop of my own, write a good-bye note to Flo, she isn't a bad old bitch, I doubled her trade since I been there, she's going to miss me, poor Flo, then leave my passkey and cut back to my trailer and pack like lightning and move on to . . .

BILL: . . . Where?

LEONA: Where I go next. You won't know, but you'll know I went fast.

[*Now she forgets her stated intention of going out of the bar and crosses to the table taken by the young man and the boy.*

[*The boy, Bobby, wears faded jeans and a sweatshirt on the back of which is lettered "Iowa to Mexico." The young man, Quentin, is dressed effetely in a yachting jacket, maroon linen slacks, and a silk neck-scarf. Despite this costume, he has a quality of sexlessness, not effeminacy. Some years ago, he must have been remarkably handsome. Now his face seems to have been burned thin by a fever that is not of the flesh.*]

LEONA: [*suddenly very amiable*]: Hi, boys!

QUENTIN: Oh. Hello. Good Evening.

BOBBY [*with shy friendliness*]: Hello.

[*Bill is grinning and chuckling. Violet's weeping in the ladies' room no longer seems to interest anyone in the bar.*]

LEONA [*to Bobby*]: How's the corn growing out there where the tall corn grows?

BOBBY: Oh, it's still growing tall.

LEONA: Good for the corn. What town or city are you from in Iowa?

**26**

BOBBY: Goldenfield. It's close to Dubuque.

LEONA: Dubuque, no shoot? I could recite the telephone book of Dubuque, but excuse me a minute, I want to play a selection on the number selector, and I'll come right back to discuss Dubuque with you. Huh? [*She moves as if totally pacified to the juke box and removes some coins from a pocket. They fall to the floor. She starts to bend over to pick them up, then decides not to bother, gives them a slight kick, gets a dollar bill out of a pocket, calling out:*] Monk, gimme change for a buck. [*Leona crosses to Monk at bar, waving a dollar bill.*]

QUENTIN: Barman? . . . Barman? . . . What's necessary to get the barman's attention here, I wonder.

[*Leona crosses back to juke box, stage right. Bobby hands Leona the change he's picked up off the floor. She looks for a number on the juke box.*]

MONK: I heard you. You've come in the wrong place. You're looking for the Jungle Bar, half a mile up the beach.

QUENTIN: Does that mean you'd rather not serve us?

MONK: Let me see the kid's draft card.

BOBBY: I just want a Coke.

QUENTIN: He wants a plain Coca-Cola, I'd like a vodka and tonic.

[*Leona lights up the juke box with a coin and selects a violin number, "Souvenir." A look of ineffable sweetness appears on her face, at the first note of music.*]

BILL: Y' can't insult 'em, there's no way to bring 'em down except to beat 'em and roll 'em.

[*The bar starts to dim, and a special spot comes up on Bill. The violin music on the juke box plays softly under.*]

**27**

I noticed him stop at the door before he come in. He was about to go right back out when he caught sight of me. Then he decided to stay. A piss-elegant one like that is asking for it. After a while, say about fifteen minutes, I'll go in the gents' and he'll follow me in there for a look at Junior. Then I'll have him hooked. He'll ask me to meet him outside by his car or at the White Castle. It'll be a short wait and I don't think I'll have t'do more than scare him a little. I don't like beating 'em up. They can't help the way they are. Who can? Not me. Left home at fifteen, and like Leona says, I've never done a lick of work in my life and I never plan to, not as long as Junior keeps batting on the home team, but my time with Leona's run out. She means to pull out of here and I mean to stay . . .

[*The bar is relighted. Leona is still at the juke box. She is leaning against the juke box, listening intently to the music.*]

MONK [*rapping at the ladies'*]: Violet, you can come out, now, she's playing that violin number.

[*Bill and Steve laugh. The bar starts to dim, and a special spot comes up on Steve. The violin number still plays under.*]

STEVE: I guess Violet's a pig, all right, and I ought to be ashamed to go around with her. But a man unmarried, forty-seven years old, employed as a short-order cook at a salary he can barely get by on alone, he can't be choosy. Nope, he has to be satisfied with the Goddam scraps in this world, and Violet's one of those scraps. She's a pitiful scrap, but . . . [*He shrugs sadly and lifts the beer bottle to his mouth.*] . . . something's better than nothing and I had nothing before I took up with her. She gave me a clap once and tried to tell me I got it off a toilet seat. I asked the doctor, is it possible to get a clap off a public toilet seat, and he said, yes, you can get it that way but you *don't*. [*He grins sadly and drinks again, wobbling slightly.*] . . . Oh, my life, my miserable, cheap life! It's like a bone thrown to a dog! I'm the dog, she's the bone. Hell, I know her habits.

She's always down there in that amusement arcade when I go to pick her up, she's down there as close as she can get to some Navy kid, playing a pinball game, and one hand is out of sight. Hustling? I reckon that's it. I know I don't provide for her, just buy her a few beers here, and a hot dog on the way home. But, Bill, why's he let her mess around with him? One night he was braggin' about the size of his tool, he said all he had to do to make a living was wear tight pants on the street. Life! . . . Throw it to a dog. I'm not a dog, I don't want it. I think I'll sit at the bar and pay no attention to her when she comes out . . .

[*The light in the bar comes up to normal level as the spot fades out. After a moment, Violet comes out of the ladies' room slowly, with a piteous expression. She is dabbing her nostrils with a bit of toilet tissue. Her lips are pursed in sorrow so that she is like travesty of a female saint under torture. She gasps and draws back a little at the sight of Leona; then, discreetly sobbing, she edges onto a bar stool, and Monk gives her a beer. Steve glares at her. She avoids looking at him. Bill grins and chuckles at his table. Leona ignores the fact that Violet has emerged from her retreat. She goes on pacing the bar, but is enthralled by the music.*]

LEONA: My God, what an instrument, it's like a thing in your heart, it's a thing that's sad but better than being happy, in a . . . crazy drunk way . . .

VIOLET: [*piteously*]: I don't know if I can drink, I feel sick at my stomach.

LEONA: Aw, shit, Violet. Who do you think you're kidding? You'll drink whatever is put in the reach of your paws. [*She slaps herself on the thigh with the sailor cap and laughs.*]

VIOLET: I do feel sick at my stomach.

LEONA: You're lucky you're sick at your stomach because your stomach can vomit, but when you're sick at your heart, that's

**29**

when it's awful, because your heart can't vomit the memories of your lifetime. I wish my heart could vomit, I wish my heart could throw up the heartbreaks of my lifetime, my days in a beauty shop and my nights in a trailer. It wouldn't surprise me at all if I drove up to Sausalito alone this night. With no one . . .

[*She glances at Bill, who grins and chuckles. Violet sobs piteously again. Leona gives Violet a fairly hard slap on the shoulders with her sailor's cap. Violet cries out in affected terror.*]

Shuddup, I'm not gonna hit you. Steve, take her off that bar stool and put her at a table, she's on a crying jag and it makes me sick.

STEVE [*to Violet*]: Come off it, Violet. Sit over here at a table, before you fall off the bar stool.

LEONA: She hasn't got a mark on her, not a mark, but she acts like I'd nearly kilt her, and turns to a weeping willow. But as for that ape that I put up in my trailer, I took him in because a life in a trailer, going from place to place any way the wind blows you, gets to be lonely, sometimes. But that's a mistake I'll not make again . . . knock wood! [*Knocks table top.*]

STEVE [*wishing to smooth troubled waters*]: Know what that means, to knock wood? It means to touch the wood of the true cross, Leona. [*He peers gravely and nearsightedly into Leona's face.*]

LEONA: Yeh, for luck, you need it.

MONK [*to Violet at bar*]: That's mine! Here's yours. [*She has reached out for Monk's drink.*]

STEVE: Violet, get off that stool and sit at a table.

LEONA: You got to move her. She's got to be moved.

[*Steve accepts this necessity. He supports Violet's frail, liquid figure to a table upstage, but her long, thin arm snakes out to remove Monk's drink from the bar top as she goes.*

[*The phone rings, and Monk lifts it.*]

MONK: Monk's Place . . . Doc, it's for you.

DOC [*crossing to the end of the bar*]: Thanks, Monk.

MONK: The old Doc's worked up a pretty good practice for a man in retirement.

LEONA: Retirement your ass, he was kicked out of the medical profession for performing operations when he was so loaded he couldn't tell the appendix from the gizzard.

MONK: Leona, go sit at your table.

LEONA: You want responsibility for a human life, do you?

MONK: Bill, I think she's ready to go home now.

LEONA: I'll go home when I'm ready and I'll do it alone.

BILL: I seen a circus with a polar bear in it that rode a three-wheel bicycle. That's what you make me think of tonight.

LEONA: You want to know something, McCorkle? I could beat the shit out of you.

BILL: Set down somewhere and shut up.

LEONA: I got a suggestion for you. Take this cab fare. . . [*She throws a handful of silver on the table.*] . . . And go get your stuff out of my trailer. Clear it all out, because when I go home tonight and find any stuff of yours there, I'll pitch it out of the trailer and bolt the door on you. I'm just in the right mood to do it.

BILL: Don't break my heart.

LEONA: What heart? We been in my trailer together for six months and you contributed nothing.

BILL: Shit, for six months I satisfied you in your trailer!

LEONA: You never satisfied nothing but my mother complex. Never mind, forget it, it's forgotten. Just do this. Take this quarter and punch number K-6 three times on the juke box.

BILL: Nobody wants to hear that violin number again.

LEONA: I do, I'm somebody. My brother, my young brother, played it as good if not better than Heifetz on that box. Y'know, I look at you and I ask myself a question. How does it feel to've never had anything beautiful in your life and not even know you've missed it? [*She crosses toward the juke box.*] Walking home with you some night, I've said, Bill, look at the sky, will you look at that sky? You never looked up, just grunted. In your life you've had no experiation . . . experience! Appreciation! . . . of the beauty of God in the sky, so what is your life but a bottle of, can of, glass of . . . one, two, three! [*She has punched the violin selection three times.*]

MONK: The Doc's still on the phone.

LEONA: "Souvenir" is a soft number.

[*The violin number starts to play again on the juke box.*]

DOC [*returning to the bar*]: I've got to deliver a baby. Shot of brandy.

LEONA [*returning to Bill's table*]: It wouldn't be sad if you didn't know what you missed by coming into this world and going out of it some day without ever having a sense of, experience of and memory of, a beautiful thing in your life such as I have in mine when I remember the violin of and the face of my young brother . . .

BILL: You told me your brother was a fruit.

LEONA: I told you privately something you're repeating in public with words as cheap as yourself. My brother who played this number had pernicious anemia from the age of thirteen and any fool knows a disease, a condition, like that would make any boy too weak to go with a woman, but he was so full of love he had to give it to someone like his music. And in my work, my profession as a beautician, I never seen skin or hair or eyes that could touch my brother's. His hair was a natural blond as soft as silk and his eyes were two pieces of heaven in a human face, and he played on the violin like he was making love to it. I cry! I cry! . . . No, I don't, I *don't* cry! . . . I'm proud that I've had something beautiful to remember as long as I live in my lifetime . . .

[*Violet sniffles softly.*]

When they passed around the plate for the offering at church, they'd have him play in the choir stall and he played and he looked like an angel, standing under the light through the stained glass window. Um-hummm. [*Her expression is rapt.*] . . . And people, even the tightwads, would drop paper money in the plates when he played. Yes, always before the service, I'd give him a shampoo-rinse so that his silky hair, the silkiest hair I've ever known on a human head in my lifetime as a beautician, would look like an angel's halo, touched with heavenly light. Why, people cried like I'm crying and the preacher was still choked up when he delivered the sermon. "Angels of Light," that was it, the number he played that Easter . . . [*She sings a phrase of the song.*] Emotions of people can be worse than people but sometimes better than people, yes, superior to them, and Haley had that gift of making people's emotions uplifted, superior to them! But he got weaker and weaker and thinner and thinner till one Sunday he collapsed in the choir stall, and after that he failed fast, just faded out of this world. Anemia—pernicious . . .

VIOLET [*sobbing*]: Anemia, that's what I've got!

**33**

LEONA: Don't compare yourself to him, how dare you compare yourself to him. He was too beautiful to live and so he died. Otherwise we'd be living together in my trailer. I'd train him to be a beautician, to bring out the homeliness in . . . I mean the, I mean the . . . [*She is confused for a moment. She lurches into a bar stool and knocks it over.*] I mean I'd train my young brother to lay his hands on the heads of the homely and lonely and bring some beauty out in them, at least for one night or one day or at least for an hour. We'd have our own shop, maybe two of 'em, and I wouldn't give you . . . [*She directs herself to Bill.*] . . . the time of the day, the time of the night, the time of the morning or afternoon, the sight of you never would have entered my sight to make me feel pity for you, no, noooo! [*She bends over Bill's table, resting her spread palms on it, to talk directly into his face.*] The companionship and the violin of my brother would be all I had any need for in my lifetime till my death-time! Remember this, Bill, if your brain can remember. Everyone needs! One beautiful thing! In the course of a lifetime! To save the heart from colluption!

BILL: What is "colluption," fat lady?

LEONA: *CORRUPTION!* . . . Without one beautiful thing in the course of a lifetime, it's all a death-time. A woman turns to a slob that lives with a slob, and life is disgusting to her and she's disgusting to life, and I'm just the one to . . .

BILL [*cutting in*]: If you'd rather live with a fruit . . .

LEONA: *Don't say it! Don't say it!* [*She seizes hold of a chair and raises it mightily over her head. Violet screams. Leona hurls the chair to the floor.*] Shit, he's not worth the price of a broken chair! [*Suddenly she bursts into laughter that is prodigious as her anger or even more, it's like an unleashed element of nature. Several patrons of the bar, involuntarily, laugh with her. Abruptly as it started, the laughter stops short. There is total silence except for the ocean sound outside.*]

VIOLET: Steve, love, get me a hot dog with chili and onion, huh? Or maybe a Whopper.

STEVE: Oh, now you want a Whopper, a king-size burger, now, huh? Always got your hand out for something.

VIOLET: That's a cruel injustice. [*Sobs.*]

STEVE: Stop it!

VIOLET: I'm in paiii-in!

LEONA: Look at her, not a mark on her, but says she's in pain and wants a hot dog with everything on it, and I heard on TV that the Food Administration found insect and rodent parts in some hot dogs sold lately. [*She has been stalking the bar.*] Let her have him for supper! [*Indicates Bill.*]

DOC [*rising from his bar stool*]: Well, I better be going. Somebody's about to be born at Treasure Island.

LEONA: That's my trailer court where I keep my trailer. A baby's about to be born there?

BILL: Naw, not a baby, a full-grown adult's about to be born there, and that's why the Doc had t'brace himself with a coupla shots of brandy.

DOC [*turning about on his bar stool, glass in hand*]: You can't make jokes about birth and you can't make jokes about death. They're miracles, holy miracles, both, yes, that's what both of them are, even though, now, they're usually surrounded by . . . expedients that seem to take away the dignity of them. Birth? Rubber gloves, boiled water, forceps, surgical shears. And death? . . . The wheeze of an oxygen tank, the jab of a hypodermic needle to put out the panic light in the dying-out eyes, tubes in the arms and the kidneys, absorbent cotton inserted in the rectum to hold back the bowels discharged when the . . . the *being stops.* [*During this speech the bar dims, and a special*

**35**

*spot comes up on Doc.*] . . . It's hard to see back of this cloud of . . . irreverent . . . paraphernalia. But behind them both are the holy mysteries of . . . birth and . . . death . . . They're dark as the face of a black man, yes, that's right, a Negro, yes. I've always figured that God is a black man with no light on his face, He moves in the dark like a black man, a Negro miner in the pit of a lightless coal mine, obscured completely by the . . . irrelevancies and irreverencies of public worship . . . standing to sing, kneeling to pray, sitting to hear the banalities of a preacher . . . Monk, did I give you my . . . ?

[*As light comes up in bar, the spot fades out.*]

MONK: Bag? Yeah, here. [*Monk hands a medical kit across the bar.*]

LEONA: I want to know, is nobody going to stop him from going out, in his condition, to deliver a baby? I want to know quick, or I'll stop him myself!

DOC: Thanks. And I'll have a shot of brandy to wash down a Benzedrine tablet to steady my hands.

LEONA: NOBODY, HUH?

DOC: Tonight, as I drove down Canyon Road, I noticed a clear bright star in the sky, and it was right over that trailer court, Treasure Island, where I'm going to deliver a baby. So now I know: I'm going to deliver a new Messiah tonight.

LEONA: The hell you are, you criminal, murdering quack, leggo of that bag!

[*Leona rushes Doc and snatches his bag. She starts toward the door but is blocked by one of the men; starts in another direction and is blocked again. She is then warily approached from three or four sides by Monk, Doc, Bill, and Steve as trainers approaching an angry "big cat."*]

[*All ad-lib during this, and in the lines that follow, Monk, Leona, and Doc speak almost simultaneously, while Steve keeps up a continual placating repetition of "Violet says" and "Have a beer with us, Leona."*]

[*The effect should almost suggest a quartet in opera: several voices blended but each pursuing its separate plaint.*]

MONK: Don't let her out with . . .

DOC: My bag! The instruments in that bag . . .

MONK: Steve, Bill, hold her, I can't with my . . .

DOC: Are worth and insured for . . . over two thousand! If you damage the contents of that bag . . . I'll sue you for their value and for slander!

[*Leona sits on Doc's bag at center table.*]

LEONA: I'll surrender this bag to you in a courtroom only!

DOC: Very expensive, very, very expensive.

STEVE: Look, she's sitting on Doc's bag. Violet says she's, Leona, Violet wants to, listen, listen, listen Leona, set down and have a beer with us! Violet says she . . .

VIOLET: Not at this table, no, no, I'm scared of Leona, she . . .

STEVE: Violet, shuddup. Leona? Violet's offered you to a . . . drink! Have a drink with us, Leona.

LEONA: I'll stay sitting on it till some action is taken to stop this man from illegal . . .

[*Bill squirts a mouthful of beer at her, and she immediately leaps up to strike at him fiercely with the sailor's cap. In that instant Monk seizes the bag from the chair and tosses it to Doc, who rushes out the door with it.*]

All of you are responsible! . . . If he murders a baby tonight and

**37**

the baby's mother! Is life worth nothing in here? I'm going out. I am going to make a phone call.

[*Bill makes a move to stop her.*]

Don't you *dare* to! Try to!

MONK: Who're you going to call?

STEVE: Who's she going to call?

LEONA [*to Monk*]: That's my business, strictly. I'm not gonna use your phone. [*She charges out the door, and the door is again left open on the sound of surf.*]

MONK: What's she up to?

STEVE: What's she up to, Bill?

BILL [*grinning and shrugging*]: I know what she's up to. She's gonna call the office at Treasure Island and tell 'em the Doc's comin' out there to deliver a baby.

MONK: Well, stop her, go stop her!

STEVE: Yeh, you better stop her.

BILL [*indifferently*]: She's disappeared in the fog.

MONK: She can get the Doc into serious trouble, and his condition's no better than mine is . . .

BILL: Shit, they know her too well to pay any attention to her call.

MONK: I hate to eighty-six anyone out of my place; I never have done that in the six years I've run it, but I swear to God, I . . . have to avoid . . . disturbance.

VIOLET [*plaintively*]: Last week she gave me a perm and a rinse for nothing, and then tonight she turns on me, threatens to kill me.

BILL: Aw, she blows hot and cold, dependin' on whichever way her liquor hits her.

VIOLET: She's got two natures in her. Sometimes she couldn't be nicer. A minute later she . . .

MONK [*at the telephone*]: Shut up a minute. Treasure Island? This is Monk speaking from Monk's Place . . . Yeah. Now. If you get a phone call out there from Leona Dawson, you know her, she's got a trailer out there, don't listen to her; she's on a crazy mean drunk, out to make trouble for a capable doctor who's been called by someone out there, an emergency call. So I thought I'd warn you, thank you. [*Monk hangs up the telephone.*]

[*Violet comes downstage, and the light is focused on her.*]

VIOLET: It's perfectly true that I have a room over the amusement arcade facing the pier. But it wasn't like Leona describes it. It took me a while to get it in shipshape condition because I was not a well girl when I moved in there, but I got it clean and attractive. It wasn't luxurious but it was clean and attractive and had an atmosphere to it. I don't see anything wrong with living upstairs from the amusement arcade, facing the pier. I don't have a bath or a toilet but I keep myself clean with a sponge bath at the washbasin and use the toilet in the amusement arcade. Anyhow it was a temporary arrangement, that's all it was, a temporary arrangement . . .

[*Leona returns to the bar. Bill rises quickly and walks over to the bar.*]

LEONA: One, two, button my shoe, three, four, shut the door, five, six, pick up sticks . . . [*No one speaks.*] . . . Silence, absolute silence. Am I being ostracized? [*She goes to the table of Quentin and Bobby.*] Well, boys, what went wrong?

QUENTIN: I'm afraid I don't know what you mean.

**39**

LEONA: Sure you know what I mean. You're not talking to each other, you don't even look at each other. There's some kind of tension between you. What is it? Is it guilt feelings? Embarrassment with guilt feelings?

BOBBY: I still don't know what you mean, but, uh . . .

LEONA: "But, uh" what?

QUENTIN: Don't you think you're being a little presumptuous?

LEONA: Naw, I know the gay scene. I learned it from my kid brother. He came out early, younger than this boy here. I know the gay scene and I know the language of it and I know how full it is of sickness and sadness; it's so full of sadness and sickness, I could almost be glad that my little brother died before he had time to be infected with all that sadness and sickness in the heart of a gay boy. This kid from Iowa, here, reminds me a little of how my brother was, and you, you remind me of how he might have become if he'd lived.

QUENTIN: Yes, you should be relieved he's dead, then.

[*She flops awkwardly into a chair at the table.*]

QUENTIN [*testily*]: Excuse me, won't you sit down?

LEONA: D'ya think I'm still standing up?

QUENTIN: Perhaps we took your table.

LEONA: I don't have any table. I'm moving about tonight like an animal in a zoo because tonight is the night of the death-day of my brother and . . . Look, the barman won't serve me, he thinks I'm on a mean drunk, so do me a favor, order a double bourbon and pretend it's for you. Do that, I'll love you for it, and of course I'll pay you for it.

QUENTIN [*calling out*]: Barman? I'd like a double bourbon.

MONK: If it's for the lady, I can't serve you.

**40**

[*Bill laughs heartily at the next table.*]

QUENTIN: It isn't for the lady, it's for me.

LEONA: How do you like that shit? [*She shrugs.*] Now what went wrong between you before you come in here, you can tell me and maybe I can advise you. I'm practically what they call a faggot's moll.

QUENTIN: Oh. Are you?

LEONA: Yes, I am. I always locate at least one gay bar in whatever city I'm in. I live in a home on wheels, I live in a trailer, so I been quite a few places. And have a few more to go. Now nobody's listening to us, they're involved in their own situations. What went wrong?

QUENTIN: Nothing, exactly. I just made a mistake, and he did, too.

LEONA: Oh. Mistakes. How did you make these mistakes? Nobody's listening, tell me.

QUENTIN: I passed him riding his bicycle up Canyon Road and I stopped my car and reversed it till I was right by his bike and I . . . spoke to him.

LEONA: What did you say to him?

BOBBY: Do you have to talk about it?

QUENTIN: Why not? I said: "Did you really ride that bike all the way from Iowa to the Pacific Coast," and he grinned and said, yes, he'd done that. And I said: "You must be tired?" and he said he was and I said: "Put your bike in the back seat of my car and come home with me for dinner."

LEONA: What went wrong? At dinner? You didn't *give* him the dinner?

QUENTIN: No, I gave him drinks, first, because I thought that after he'd had dinner, he might say: "Thank you, good night."

**41**

BOBBY: Let's shut up about that. I had dinner after.

LEONA: After what?

QUENTIN: After . . .

BOBBY: I guess to you people who live here it's just an old thing you're used to, I mean the ocean out there, the Pacific, it's not an *experience* to you any more like it is to me. You say it's the Pacific, but me, I say THE PACIFIC!

QUENTIN: Well, everything is in "caps" at your age, Bobby.

LEONA [*to Quentin*]: Do you work for the movies?

QUENTIN: Naturally, what else?

LEONA: Act in them, you're an actor?

QUENTIN: No. Script writer.

LEONA [*vaguely*]: Aw, you write movies, huh?

QUENTIN: Mostly rewrite. Adapt. Oh, I had a bit of a setback when they found me too literate for my first assignment . . . converting an epic into a vehicle for the producer's doxy, a grammar school dropout. But the industry is using me now to make blue movies bluer with . . . you know, touches of special . . . erotica . . . lovely.

[*Leona laughs.*]

LEONA: Name?

QUENTIN: Quentin . . . Miss? [*He rises.*]

LEONA: Leona. Dawson. And he's?

QUENTIN: Bobby.

LEONA: Bobby, come back to the party. I want you back here, love. Resume your seat. [*Resting a hand on the boy's stiff shoulder*] . . . You're a literary gent with the suede shit-kickers and a brass-button blazer and a . . . [*Flicks his scarf.*]

**42**

BILL [*leering from bar*]: Ask him if he's got change for a three-dollar bill.

QUENTIN: Yes, if you have the bill.

LEONA: Ignore the peasants. I don't think that monkey-faced mother will serve us that bourbon . . . I never left his bar without leaving a dollar tip on the table, and this is what thanks I get for it, just because it's the death-day of my brother and I showed a little human emotion about it. Now what's the trouble between you and this kid from Iowa where the tall corn blows, I mean grows?

QUENTIN: I only go for straight trade. But this boy . . . look at him! Would you guess he was gay? . . . I didn't, I thought he was straight. But I had an unpleasant surprise when he responded to my hand on his knee by putting his hand on mine.

BOBBY: I don't dig the word "*gay.*" To me they mean nothing, those words.

LEONA: Aw, you've got plenty of time to learn the meanings of words and cynical attitudes. Why he's got eyes like my brother's! Have you paid him?

QUENTIN: For disappointment?

LEONA: Don't be a mean-minded mother. Give him a five, a ten. If you picked up what you don't want, it's your mistake and pay for it.

BOBBY: I don't want money from him. I thought he was nice, I liked him.

LEONA: Your mistake, too. [*She turns to Quentin.*] Gimme your wallet.

[*Quentin hands her his wallet.*]

BOBBY: He's disappointed. I don't want anything from him.

**43**

LEONA: Don't be a fool. Fools aren't respected, you fool. [*She removes a bill from the wallet and stuffs it in the pocket of Bobby's shirt. Bobby starts to return it.*] OK, I'll hold it for you till he cuts out of here to make another pickup and remind me to give it back to you when he goes. He wants to pay you, it's part of his sad routine. It's like doing penance . . . penitence.

BILL [*loudly*]: Monk, where's the head?

MONK: None of that here, Bill.

QUENTIN [*with a twist of a smile toward Bill*]: Pity.

LEONA [*turning to Quentin*]: Do you like being alone except for vicious pickups? The kind you go for? If I understood you correctly? . . . Christ, you have terrible eyes, the expression in them! What are you looking at?

QUENTIN: The fish over the bar . . .

LEONA: You're changing the subject.

QUENTIN: No, I'm not, not a bit . . . Now suppose some night I woke up and I found that fantastic fish . . . what is it?

LEONA: Sailfish. What about it?

QUENTIN: Suppose I woke up some midnight and found that peculiar thing swimming around in my bedroom? Up the Canyon?

LEONA: In a fish bowl? Aquarium?

QUENTIN: No, not in a bowl or aquarium: free, unconfined.

LEONA: Impossible.

QUENTIN: Granted. It's impossible. But suppose it occurred just the same, as so many impossible things *do* occur just the same. Suppose I woke up and discovered it there, swimming round and round in the darkness over my bed, with a faint phosphorescent glow in its big goggle-eyes and its gorgeously iridescent fins and tail making a swishing sound as it circles around and about and around and about right over my head in my bed.

LEONA: Hah!

QUENTIN: Now suppose this admittedly preposterous thing did occur. What do you think I would say?

LEONA: To the fish?

QUENTIN: To myself and the fish.

LEONA: . . . I'll be raped by an ape if I can imagine what a person would say in a situation like that.

QUENTIN: I'll tell you what I would say, I would say: "Oh, well . . ."

LEONA: . . . Just "Oh, well"?

QUENTIN: "Oh, well" is all I would say before I went back to sleep.

LEONA: What I would say is: "Get the hell out of here, you goggle-eyed monstrosity of a mother," that's what I'd say to it.

MONK: Leona, let's lighten it up.

QUENTIN: You don't see the point of my story?

LEONA: Nope.

QUENTIN [*to Bobby*]: Do *you* see the point of my story?

[*Bobby shakes his head.*]

Well, maybe I don't either.

LEONA: Then why'd you tell it?

QUENTIN: What is the thing that you mustn't lose in this world before you're ready to leave it? The one thing you mustn't lose ever?

**45**

LEONA: . . . Love?

[*Quentin laughs.*]

BOBBY: Interest?

QUENTIN: That's closer, much closer. Yes, that's almost it. The word that I had in mind is surprise, though. The capacity for being surprised. I've lost the capacity for being surprised, so completely lost it, that if I woke up in my bedroom late some night and saw that fantastic fish swimming right over my head, I wouldn't be really surprised.

LEONA: You mean you'd think you were dreaming?

QUENTIN: Oh, no. Wide awake. But not really surprised. [*The special spot concentrates on him. The bar dims, but an eerie glow should remain on the sailfish over the bar.*] There's a coarseness, a deadening coarseness, in the experience of most homosexuals. The experiences are quick, and hard, and brutal, and the pattern of them is practically unchanging. Their act of love is like the jabbing of a hypodermic needle to which they're addicted but which is more and more empty of real interest and surprise. This lack of variation and surprise in their . . . "love life" . . . [*He smiles harshly.*] . . . spreads into other areas of . . . "sensibility?" [*He smiles again.*] . . . Yes, once, quite a long while ago, I was often startled by the sense of being alive, of being *myself, living!* Present on earth, in the flesh, yes, for some completely mysterious reason, a single, separate, intensely conscious being, *myself: living!* . . . Whenever I would feel this . . . *feeling,* this . . . shock of . . . what? . . . self-realization? . . . I would be stunned, I would be thunderstruck by it. And by the existence of everything that exists, I'd be lightning-struck with astonishment . . . it would do more than astound me, it would give me a feeling of panic, the sudden sense of . . . I suppose it was like an epileptic seizure, except that I didn't fall to the ground in convulsions; no, I'd be more apt to try to lose myself in a crowd on a street until

**46**

the seizure was finished . . . They were dangerous seizures. One time I drove into the mountains and smashed the car into a tree, and I'm not sure if I *meant* to do that, or . . . In a forest you'll sometimes see a giant tree, several hundred years old, that's scarred, that's blazed by lightning, and the wound is almost obscured by the obstinately still living and growing bark. I wonder if such a tree has learned the same lesson that I have, not to feel astonishment any more but just go on, continue for two or three hundred years more? . . . This boy I picked up tonight, the kid from the tall corn country, still has the capacity for being surprised by what he sees, hears and feels in this kingdom of earth. All the way up the canyon to my place, he kept saying, *I can't believe it, I'm here, I've come to the Pacific, the world's greatest ocean!* . . . as if nobody, Magellan or Balboa or even the Indians had ever seen it before him; yes, like he'd discovered this ocean, the largest on earth, and so now, because he'd found it himself, it existed, now, for the first time, never before . . . And this excitement of his reminded me of my having lost the ability to say: "My God!" instead of just: "Oh, well." I've asked all the questions, shouted them at deaf heaven, till I was hoarse in the voice box and blue in the face, and gotten no answer, not the whisper of one, nothing at all, you see, but the sun coming up each morning and going down that night, and the galaxies of the night sky trooping onstage like chorines, robot chorines: one, two, three, kick, one two, three, kick . . . Repeat any question too often and what do you get, what's given? . . . A big carved rock by the desert, a . . . monumental symbol of worn-out passion and bewilderment in you, a stupid stone paralyzed sphinx that knows no answers that you don't but comes on like the oracle of all time, waiting on her belly to give out some outcries of universal wisdom, and if she woke up some midnight at the edge of the desert and saw that fantastic fish swimming over her head . . . y'know what she'd say, too? She'd say: "Oh, well" . . . and go back to sleep for another five thousand years. [*He turns back; and the bar is relighted. He returns to the table*

**47**

*and adjusts his neck-scarf as he speaks to Bobby.*] . . . Your bicycle's still in my car. Shall I put it on the sidewalk?

BOBBY: I'll go get it.

QUENTIN: No. You will find it here, by the door. [*Desires no further exposure to Bobby.*]

LEONA [*to Bobby*]: Stay here awhile . . . Set down. He wants to escape.

BOBBY: From me? [*Meaning "Why?"*]

LEONA [*visibly enchanted by Bobby, whom she associates with her lost brother*]: Maybe more from himself. Stay here awhile.

BOBBY: . . . It's . . . late for the road. [*But he may resume his seat here.*]

LEONA: On a bike, yeh, too late, with the dreaded fog people out. Y'know, I got a suggestion. It's sudden but it's terrific. [*She leans across the table, urgently.*] Put your bike in my trailer. It's got two bunks.

BOBBY: Thank you but . . .

LEONA: It wouldn't cost you nothing and we'd be company for each other. My trailer's not ordinary, it's a Fonda deluxe, stereo with two speakers, color TV with an eight-inch screen, toucha-matic, and baby, you don't look well fed. I'm a hell of a cook, could qualify as a pro in that line, too.

BILL [*to Steve*]: What a desperate pitch. I was the wrong sex. She wants a fruit in her stinkin' trailer.

LEONA: Nothing stunk in my trailer but what's out now . . . He can't understand a person wanting to give protection to another, it's past his little reception. [*To Bobby*] Why're you staring out into space with visibility zero?

**48**

BOBBY [*slowly, with a growing ardor*]: I've got a lot of important things to think over alone, new things. I feel new vibes, vibrations, I've got to sort out alone.

LEONA: Mexico's a dangerous country for you, and there's lonely stretches of road . . . [*She's thinking of herself, too.*]

BOBBY [*firmly but warmly to her*]: Yes . . . I need that, now.

LEONA: Baby, are you scared I'd put the make on you?

[*Bill grunts contemptuously but with the knowledge that he is now truly evicted.*]

I don't, like they say, come on heavy . . . never, not with . . . [*She lightly touches Bobby's hand on the table.*] *This* is my touch! Is it *heavy?*

[*Bobby rises. Quentin is seen dimly, setting the bicycle at the door.*]

BOBBY: That man didn't come on heavy. [*Looking out at Quentin.*] His hand on my knee was just a human touch and it seemed natural to me to return it.

LEONA: Baby, his hand had . . . ambitions . . . And, oh, my God, you've got the skin and hair of my brother and even almost the eyes!

BILL: Can he play the fiddle?

BOBBY: In Goldenfield, Iowa, there was a man like that, ran a flower shop with a back room, decorated Chinese, with incense and naked pictures, which he invited boys into. I heard about it. Well, things like that aren't tolerated for long in towns like Goldenfield. There's suspicion and talk and then public outrage and action, and he had to leave so quick he didn't clear out the shop. [*The bar lights have faded out, and the special spot illuminates Bobby.*] A bunch of us entered one night. The drying-up flowers rattled in the wind and the wind-chimes tinkled and

**49**

the . . . naked pictures were just . . . pathetic, y'know. Except for a sketch of Michelangelo's David. I don't think anyone noticed me snatch it off the wall and stuff it into my pocket. Dreams . . . images . . . nights . . . On the plains of Nebraska I passed a night with a group of runaway kids my age and it got cold after sunset. A lovely wild young girl invited me under a blanket with just a smile, and then a boy, me between, and both of them kept saying "love," one of 'em in one ear and one in the other, till I didn't know which was which "love" in which ear or which . . . touch . . . The plain was high and the night air . . . exhilarating and the touches not heavy . . . The man with the hangup has set my bike by the door. [*Extends his hand to Leona. The bar is relighted.*] It's been a pleasure to meet a lady like you. Oh, I've got a lot of new adventures, experiences, to think over alone on my speed iron. I think I'll drive all night, I don't feel tired. [*Bobby smiles as he opens the door and nods good-bye to Monk's Place.*]

LEONA: Hey, Iowa to Mexico, the money . . . here's the money! [*She rushes to the door, but Bobby is gone with his bicycle.*]

BILL: He don't want a lousy five bucks, he wants everything in the wallet. He'll roll the faggot and hop back on his bike looking sweet and innocent as her brother fiddling in church.

[*Leona rushes out, calling.*]

STEVE: The Coast is overrun with 'em, they come running out here like animals out of a brushfire.

MONK [*as he goes to each table, collecting the empty cans and bottles, emptying ash trays on a large serving tray*]: I've got no moral objections to them as a part of humanity, but I don't encourage them here. One comes in, others follow. First thing you know you're operating what they call a gay bar and it sounds like a bird cage, they're standing three deep at the bar and lining up at the men's room. Business is terrific for a few months. Then in comes the law. The place is raided, the boys hauled off in the wagon, and your place is padlocked. And then a cop or gangster pays you a social visit, big smile, all buddy-buddy. You had a good thing going, a real swinging place, he tells you, but you needed protection. He offers you protection and you buy it. The place is reopened and business is terrific a few months more. And then? It's raided again, and the next time it's reopened, you pay out of your nose, your ears, and your ass. Who wants it? I don't want it. I want a small steady place that I can handle alone, that brings in a small, steady profit. No buddy-buddy association with gangsters and the police. I want to know the people that come in my place so well I can serve them their brand of liquor or beer before they name it, soon as they come in the door. And all their personal problems, I want to know that, too.

[*Violet begins to hum softly, swaying to and fro like a water plant.*

[*When Monk finishes cleaning off the tables, he returns behind the bar. The bar lights dim, and his special spot comes up.*]

I'm fond of, I've got an affection for, a sincere interest in my regular customers here. They send me post cards from wherever they go and tell me what's new in their lives and I am interested in it. Just last month one of them I hadn't seen in about five years, he died in Mexico City and I was notified of the death and that he'd willed me all he owned in the world, his personal effects and a two-hundred-fifty-dollar savings account in a bank. A thing like that is beautiful as music. These things, these people, take the place of a family in my life. I love to come down those steps from my room to open the place for the evening, and when I've closed for the night, I love climbing back up those steps with my can of Ballantine's ale, and the stories, the jokes, the confidences and confessions I've heard that night,

**51**

it makes me feel not alone . . . I've had heart attacks, and I'd be a liar to say they didn't scare me and don't still scare me. I'll die some night up those steps, I'll die in the night alone, and I hope it don't wake me up, that I just slip away, quietly.

[*Leona has returned. The light in the bar comes up but remains at a low level.*]

LEONA: . . . Is there a steam engine in here? Did somebody drive in here on a steam engine while I was out?

MONK [*returning from his meditation*]: . . . Did what?

LEONA: I hear something going huff-huff like an old locomotive pulling into a station. [*She is referring to a sound like a panting dog. It comes from Bill at the unlighted table where Violet is seated between him and Steve.*] . . . Oh, well, my home is on wheels . . . Bourbon sweet, Monk.

MONK: Leona, you don't need another.

LEONA: Monk, it's after midnight, my brother's death-day is over, I'll be all right, don't worry. [*She goes to the bar.*] . . . It was selfish of me to wish he was still alive.

[*A pin-spot of light picks up Violet's tear-stained and tranced face at the otherwise dark table.*]

. . . She's got some form of religion in her hands . . .

CURTAIN

*An hour later. "Group singing" is in progress at the table stage right. Leona is not participating. She is sitting moodily at the bar facing front.*

VIOLET: "I don't want to set the world on fii-yuh."

STEVE: "I don't want to set the world on fii-yuh."

VIOLET: I like old numbers best. Here's an oldie that I learned from my mother. [*She rises and assumes a sentimental look.*]
"Lay me where sweet flowers blos-sóm,
Where the dainty lily blows
Where the pinks and violets min-gle,
Lay me underneath the rose."

LEONA: Shit. Y'don't need a rose to lay her, you could lay her under a cactus and she wouldn't notice the diff-rence.

[*Bill crosses to the bar for a beer.*]

I guess you don't think I'm serious about it, hitting the highway tonight.

[*Bill shrugs and crosses to a downstage table.*]

Well, I am, I'm serious about it. [*She sits at his table.*] An experienced expert beautician can always get work anywhere.

BILL: Your own appearance is a bad advertisement for your line of work.

LEONA: I don't care how I look as long as I'm clean and decent . . . and *self-supporting.* When I haul into a new town, I just look through the yellow pages of the telephone directory and pick out a beauty shop that's close to my trailer camp. I go to the shop and offer to work a couple of days for nothing, and after that couple of days I'm in like Flynn, and on my own terms, which is fifty per cent of charges for all I do, and my tips,

**53**

of course, too. They like my work and they like my personality, my approach to customers. I keep them laughing.

BILL: You keep me laughing, too.

LEONA: . . . Of course, there's things about you I'll remember with pleasure, such as waking up sometimes in the night and looking over the edge of the upper bunk to see you asleep in the lower. [*Bill leaves the table. She raises her voice to address the bar-at-large.*] Yeah, he slept in the lower 'cause when he'd passed out or nearly, it would of taken a derrick to haul him into the upper bunk. So I gave him the lower bunk and took the upper myself.

BILL: As if you never pass out. Is that the idea you're selling?

LEONA: When I pass out I wake up in a chair or on the floor, oh, no, the floor was good enough for me in your opinion, and sometimes you stepped on me even, yeah, like I was a rug or a bug, because your nature is selfish. You think because you've lived off one woman after another woman after eight or ten women you're something superior, special. Well, you're special but not superior, baby. I'm going to worry about you after I've gone and I'm sure as hell leaving tonight, fog or no fog on the highway, but I'll worry about you because you refuse to grow up and that's a mistake that you make, because you can only refuse to grow up for a limited period in your lifetime and get by with it . . . I *loved* you! . . . I'm not going to cry. It's only being so tired that makes me cry.

[*Violet starts weeping for her.*]

VIOLET: Bill, get up and tell Leona good-bye. She's a lonely girl without a soul in the world.

LEONA: I've got the world in the world, and McCorkle don't have to make the effort to get himself or any part of him up, it's easier to stay down. And as for being lonely, listen, ducks,

**54**

that applies to every mother's son and daughter of us alive, we were given warning of that before we were born almost, and yet . . . When I come to a new place, it takes me two or three weeks, that's all it takes me, to find somebody to live with in my home on wheels and to find a night spot to hang out in. Those first two or three weeks are rough, sometimes I wish I'd stayed where I was before, but I know from experience that I'll find somebody and locate a night spot to booze in, and get acquainted with . . . friends . . . [*The light has focused on her. She moves downstage with her hands in her pockets, her face and voice very grave as if she were less confident that things will be as she says.*] And then, all at once, something wonderful happens. All the past disappointments in people I left behind me, just disappear, evaporate from my mind, and I just remember the good things, such as their sleeping faces, and . . . Life! Life! I never just said, "Oh, well," I've always said "Life!" to life, like a song to God, too, because I've lived in my lifetime and not been afraid of . . . changes . . . [*She goes back to the bar.*] . . . However, y'see, I've got this pride in my nature. When I live with a person I love and care for in my life, I expect his respect, and when I see I've lost it, I GO, GO! . . . So a home on wheels is the only right home for me.

[*Violets starts toward Leona.*]

What is she doing here?

[*Violet has weaved to the bar.*]

Hey! What are *you* doing here?

VIOLET: You're the best friend I ever had, the best friend I . . . [*She sways and sobs like a* religieuse *in the grip of a vision.*]

LEONA: What's that, what're you saying?

[*Violet sobs.*]

She can't talk. What was she saying?

VIOLET: . . . BEST . . . !

LEONA: WHAT?

VIOLET: . . . *Friend!*

LEONA: I'd go further than that, I'd be willing to bet I'm the *only* friend that you've had, and the next time you come down sick nobody will bring you nothing, no chicken, no hot beef bouillon, no chinaware, no silver, and no interest and concern about your condition, and you'll die in your rattrap with no human voice, just bang, bang, bang from the bowling alley and billiards. And when you die you should feel a relief from the conditions you lived in. Now I'm leaving you two suffering, bleeding hearts together, I'm going to sit at the bar. I had a Italian boy friend that taught me a saying, *"Meglior solo que mal accompanota,"* which means that you're better alone than in the company of a bad companion.

[*She starts to the bar, as Doc enters.*]

Back already, huh? It didn't take you much time to deliver the baby. Or did you bury the baby? Or did you bury the mother? Or did you bury them both, the mother and baby?

DOC [*to Monk*]: Can you shut up this woman?

LEONA: Nobody can shut up this woman. Quack, quack, quack, Doctor Duck, quack, quack, quack, quack, quack!

DOC: I'M A LICENSED PHYSICIAN!

LEONA: SHOW *me your license. I'll shut up when I see it!*

DOC: A doctor's license to practice isn't the size of a drunken driver's license, you don't put it in a wallet, you hang it on the wall of your office.

LEONA: Here is your office! Which wall is your license hung on? Beside the sailfish or where? Where is your license to practice hung up, in the gents', with other filthy scribbles?!

**56**

MONK: Leona, you said your brother's death-day was over and I thought you meant you were . . .

LEONA: THOUGHT I MEANT I WAS *WHAT?*

MONK: You were ready to cool it. BILL! . . . Take Leona home, now.

LEONA: Christ, do you think I'd let him come near me?! Or near my trailer?! Tonight?! [*She slaps the bar several times with her sailor cap, turning to the right and left as if to ward off assailants, her great bosom heaving, a jungle-look in her eyes.*]

VIOLET: Steve, if we don't go now the King-burger stand will shut on us, and I've had nothing but liquids on my stomach all day. So I need a Whopper tonight.

[*Bill laughs.*]

STEVE: You'll get a hot dog with chili and everything on the way home. Get me . . . get me . . . get me. Grab and grope. You disgrace me! . . . your habits.

VIOLET: You're underdeveloped and you blame me.

LEONA [*looking out*]: Yes . . . [*She slaps something with her cap.*] *Yes!*

VIOLET: What did she mean by that? Another sarcastic crack?

LEONA: When I say "yes" it is not sarcacstic . . . It means a decision to act.

MONK: The place is closing so will everybody get themselves together now, please.

VIOLET: I do have to have something solid. Too much liquids and not enough solids in the system upsets the whole system. Ask the Doc if it don't. Doc don't it upset the system, liquids without solids? All day long?

**57**

[*Doc has been sunk in profoundly dark and private reflections. He emerges momentarily to reply to Violet's direct question.*]

DOC: If that's a professional question to a doctor whose office is here . . . [*A certain ferocity is boiling in him and directed mostly at himself.*] My fee is . . . another brandy. [*He turns away with a short, disgusted laugh.*]

MONK: Something wrong, Doc?

[*Violet has crossed to Bill, as a child seeking protection.*]

DOC: Why, no, what could be wrong? But a need to put more liquid in my system . . .

LEONA [*convulsively turning about*]: Yes . . . yes! [*This no longer relates to anything but her private decision.*]

BILL [*to himself*]: I'm not about to spend the night on the beach . . .

VIOLET: [*leaning toward Bill*]: I am not neither, so why don't we check in somewhere? Us, two, together?

STEVE: I heard that.

LEONA: Yes . . . yes!

MONK: I said the place is closing.

VIOLET: Let's go together, us three, and talk things over at the King-burger stand.

STEVE: Being a cook I know the quality of those giant hamburgers called Whoppers, and they're fit only for dog food.

VIOLET: I think we better leave, now. [*Extends her delicate hands to both men.*] Steve? Bill? [*They all rise unsteadily and prepare to leave.*] Bill, you know I feel so protected now. [*Violet, Steve, and Bill start out.*]

LEONA [*stomping the floor with a powerful foot*]: Y' WANT YOUR ASS IN A SLING? BEFORE YOU'RE LAID UNDER THAT ROSE?

VIOLET [*shepherded past Leona by Steve and Bill*]: If we don't see you again, good luck wherever you're going.

[*They go out the door.*]

LEONA [*rushing after them*]: That's what she wants, she wants her ass in a sling!

[*She rushes out the door. A moment or two later, as Monk looks out, and above the boom of the surf, Violet's histrionically shrill outcries are heard. This is followed by an off-stage quarrel between Leona and a night watchman on the beach. Their overlapping, ad-lib dialogue continues in varying intensity as background to the business on stage: "If you don't settle down and come along peaceful-like, I'm going to call the wagon! . . ." "Do that, I just dare you to do it— go on, I just dare you to call the wagon! I want to ride in a wagon—it's got wheels, hasn't it—I'll ride any Goddam thing on wheels! . . ." "Oh, no—listen, lady, what's your name anyhow? . . ." "I'm just the one to do it! . . . I tell you my name? I'm going to tell you my name? What's your name? I want your name! Oh boy, do I want your name! . . ." "Listen, please, come on, now, let's take this thing easy . . ." "I've been drinking in this bar, and it's not the first time you . . ." "Let's go! You raise hell every night! . . ." "Every night! This isn't the first time—I've been meaning to report you! Yes, I'm going to report you! Yes, how's that for a switch? . . ." "I'm just trying to do my duty! . . ." "I live in a home on wheels, and every night you try to molest me when I come home! . . ." "No! You're wrong—you're always in there drinking and raising hell and . . ." "Yeah, but you let criminals go free, right? . . ." "No, I don't! . . ." "People can't walk in the street, murdering, robbing, thieving, and all I do is*]

**59**

*have a few Goddam drinks, just because it's my brother's death-day, so I was showing a little human emotion—take your hands off me! . . ." "Come on now! . . ." "Don't you put your hands on a lady like me! . . ." "No, I'm not! . . ." "I'm a Goddam lady! That's what I am, and you just lay off! . . ." "I've had enough of this! . . ." "Every night I come out here, you're looking for free drinks, that's what's the matter with you! . . ." "I've never had a drink in my life, lady! . . ." "You never had a drink in your life! . . ." "No, I haven't, I've . . ." "Show me your identification, that's what I want to see! . . ." "I'm just trying to do my duty . . ." "Look here, old man . . ." "I don't know why I have to put up with an old dame like you this way . . ." "Oh!—Oh!—Why you Goddam son of a! . . ." "Now! . . ." "Don't you talk to me like that . . ." "I'm not talking to you, I'm telling you to come over here and let me get you to the telephone here! . . ." "You've been harassing that man Monk! . . ." "I'm not harassing any- body! . . ." "You're not harassing anybody? . . ." "You come over to this Monk's Place every night and raise hell, the whole damn bunch of you, and a poor man like me trying to earn a few dollars and make a living for his old woman and . . ." "Let me see your identification! What precint are you from? . . ." "Oh, yeah . . ." "Go on, I want that identification, and I want that uniform off you, and that badge . . ." "You won't do anything of the sort! . . ." "Oh, yeah . . ." "Yes, I'm doing my job, what I'm doing is legal! . . ." "I happen to have more influence up at that station than you . . . Goddam pig! . . ." "I haven't done nothing to you, I'm just trying to do my job . . ." "Do your job? . . ." "Yes, and you're giving me a lot of hard time! . . ." "There's raping and thieving and criminals and robbers walking the streets, breaking store fronts, break- ing into every bar . . ." "Well, that's not my—listen, lady! I'm just the night watchman around this beach here. I'm just on the beach nights, I don't have anything to do with what's going on somewhere else in the city, just on this beach! . . ."*

"*You don't know what's going on on the beach* . . ." "*I know what's going on on the beach, and it's you and that crowd drinking every night, raising hell!* . . ." "*We're not raising hell every night!* . . ." "*If I was your husband, golly, I—I—by God I would take care of you, I wouldn't put up with your likes, you and that crowd drinking every night!* . . ." "*I like that uniform you've got on you, and I'm gonna have it!* . . ." "*Why do you have to pick on a little man like me for?* . . ." "*I've seen you sneaking around, Peeping Tom, that's what you are!* . . ." "*No, that's not so!* . . ." "*I've seen you sneaking around looking in ladies' windows* . . ." "*That's not true! I'm just trying to do my duty! I keep telling you* . . ." "*Yeah, peeping in windows* . . ." "*No!* . . ." "*Watching people undress* . . ." "*No! You* . . ." "*I've seen you, you lascivious old man!* . . ." "*I've seen you taking these young men over to your trailer court and making studs out of them!* . . ." "*Yeah!—Yeah!— Yeah! Men, that's what I take to my trailer! I wouldn't take a palsied old man like you!* . . ." "*You know damn well I wasn't trying to get you to* . . . *! I was trying to get you to this telephone box, where I was going to!* . . ." "*You will not be able to, old man!* . . ." "*Listen, Miss, I asked you to give me your identification! You give me your identification so I can tell who you are!* . . ." "*I want* your *identification! I've seen you, I've seen you sneaking around the trailer court, I've seen you looking in windows* . . ." "*Oh, that's a lie! I never did a thing like that in all my life, I go to church. I'm a good Christian man!* . . ." "*Oh yeah! Yeah! Yeah!* . . ." "*I could take you in if I were younger, I wouldn't* have *to call the highway patrol, but I'm going to do that right now!* . . ." "*Listen, Holy Willie! I've seen your likes in church before! I wouldn't trust you with a* . . ." "*A little church wouldn't do you any harm neither!* . . ." "*Old man* . . . *Yeah! Yeah!* . . ." "*I've seen you with those young studs!* . . ." "*Doesn't that make you excited?* . . ." "*No, by God, it doesn't!* . . ." "*Is that your problem?* . . ." "*No, I don't have none! You're the one with* *the hang-ups and problems—you are a problem! You hang out here all night in that damn Monk's Place! . . ." "I've got my own man, I don't have to worry about any other man, I got my own man in my trailer! . . ." "Anyone want to spend the night with you, he must be a pig then, he must be some kind of pig living with you! . . ." "Fat old bag of wind, don't you talk to me! . . ." "Look, I'm tired of talking to you, by God, I've put up with you all I'm going to! I told you I was going to call the highway patrol! . . ." "I've seen the way you look at me when you . . ." "That's a lie!—I never . . ." "Yeah! Yeah! . . ." "I—I . . ." "I've seen you skulking around in the dark, looking in windows! . . ." "I don't need your kind! I've got a good woman at home, and she takes care of me, she takes good care of me! If I can get this job done and you'll just settle down and be quiet, we wouldn't have all this noise! . . ." "Does your wife know about the girls you go out with? . . ." "You're trying to incriminate me! . . ." "Does she know about that? . . ." "I know what you're trying to do . . ." "I've seen you . . ." "Trying to get me in trouble! Trying to get me to lose my job here! . . ." "I know what you holy boys are like! . . ." "Why don't you go back in there and raise some more hell with those young studs? . . ." "I ain't doing that neither . . ." "If you'd be quiet! . . ." "Stop harassing! . . ." "I ain't harassing nothing! . . ." "Every time you want a drink, yes? . . ." "I don't, I don't . . ."*]

MONK [*to Doc*]: Goddam, she's left her suitcase.

DOC [*musing darkly*]: . . . Done what?

MONK: She's left that bag in here, which means she's coming back.

DOC: Aw, yeah, a guarantee of it, she's going to provide you with the solace of her companionship up those stairs to the living quarters. [*He faces out from the bar.*] Y'know, that narrow flight of stairs is like the uterine passage to life, and I'd say that strange, that amorphous-looking creature is expecting to enter the world up the uterine passage to your living quarters above. [*He rises, chuckling darkly.*] Is the toilet repaired in the gents' room?

MONK [*listening to noises outside*]: Yeh, plumber fixed it today.

[*Doc sighs and lumbers heavily the way pointed by the chalk-white hand signed "GENTS" off stage right.*]

[*Monk crosses to the door to assess the disturbance outside. Bill rushes into the bar.*]

BILL: For Chrissake, get an ambulance with a strait jacket for her.

MONK: You mean you can't hold her, you stupid prick?

BILL: No man can hold that woman when she goes ape. Gimme a dime, I'm gonna call the Star of the Sea psycho ward.

MONK: Don't put a hand on that phone.

[*Violet now rushes in the door. She continues her histrionic outcries.*]

VIOLET: They're callin' the wagon for her, she's like a wild thing out there, lock the door, don't let her at me. Hide me, help me! Please! [*She rushes toward the stairs.*]

MONK: Stay down those stairs, pick up your luggage, I'll . . . I'll . . . call a taxi for you.

VIOLET: Steve done nothin' to . . . nothin' . . . Just run!

[*Altercation rises outside. Violet rushes into the ladies'. Monk closes the door and bolts it. Doc returns from the gents', putting on his jacket. His pant cuffs are wet.*]

DOC: The toilet still overflows.

[*Steve calls at the locked door.*]

STEVE: Vi'let? Monk?

[*Monk admits him. Steve enters with a confused look about, two dripping hot dogs in his hand.*]

STEVE: Vi'let, is Vi'let, did Vi'let get back in here?

MONK: Yeh, she's back in the ladies'. [*Monk closes door.*]

STEVE [*shuffling rapidly to the ladies'*]: Vi'let? Vi'let? Hear me?

MONK: No. She don't.

STEVE: Vi'let, the King-burger's closed. So I couldn't get a Whopper . . . I got you two dogs, with chili and sauerkraut. You can come out now, Leona's getting arrested. Violet screamed for help to a cop that hates and hassles me ev'ry time I go home.

MONK: Those dogs you're holding are dripping on the floor.

DOC: Committing a nuisance . . .

STEVE: Vi'let, the dogs'll turn cold, the chili's dripping off 'em. You can't stay all night in a toilet, Vi'let.

VIOLET [*from the ladies'*]: I can, I will, go away.

STEVE: She says she's gonna stay all night in a toilet. Wow . . . I mean . . . wow. [*Starts eating one of the hot dogs with a slurping sound.*]

MONK: If she's called the law here I want her to shut up in there.

STEVE: Vi'let, shut up in there. Come out for your dog.

VIOLET: Take your dog away and leave me alone. You give me no protection and no support a'tall.

**64**

[*Doc utters a laugh that is dark with an ultimate recognition of human absurdity and his own self-loathing.*]

MONK: [*touching his chest*]: . . . Doc? . . . Have a nightcap with me.

DOC: Thanks, Monk, I could use one.

MONK [*leaning back in chair and tapping his upper abdomen*]: Angina or gastritis, prob'ly both.

DOC: In that location, it's gas.

MONK: What happened at Treasure Island?

DOC [*sipping his "shot"*]: Tell you when I . . . get this . . . down.

BILL: Time . . . runs out with one and you go to another. Got a call from a woman guv'ment employee in Sacramento. She's got a co-op in a high-rise condominium, lives so high on the hog with payoffs an' all she can't see ground beneath her.

MONK: Why're you shouting, at who?

BILL: Nobody's ever thrown McCorkle out.

MONK: Unusual and not expected things can happen.

[*Leona is heard from off stage: "Okay, you make your phone call, and I'll make mine."*]

So, Doc, how'd it go at the trailer camp?

[*He and Doc are seated in profile at the downstage table. Steve and Bill are silhouetted at the edge of the lighted area.*]

DOC: The birth of the baby was at least three months premature, so it was born dead, of course, and just beginning to look like a human baby . . . The man living with the woman in the trailer said, "Don't let her see it, get it out of the trailer." I agreed with the man that she shouldn't see it, so I put this fetus

**65**

in a shoe box . . . [*He speaks with difficulty, as if compelled to.*]
The trailer was right by the beach, the tide was coming in with
heavy surf, so I put the shoe box . . . and contents . . . where
the tide would take it.

MONK: . . . Are you sure that was legal?

DOC: Christ, no, it wasn't legal . . . I'd barely set the box down
when the man came out shouting for me. The woman had started
to hemorrhage. When I went back in the trailer, she was bleeding to death. The man hollered at me, "Do something, can't you
do something for her!"

MONK: . . . Could you?

DOC: . . . I could have told the man to call an ambulance for
her, but I thought of the probable consequences to me, and
while I thought about that, the woman died. She was a small
woman, but not small enough to fit in a shoe box, so I . . .
I gave the man a fifty-dollar bill that I'd received today for performing an abortion. I gave it to him in return for his promise
not to remember my name . . . [*He reaches for the bottle. His
hand shakes so that he can't refill his shot-glass. Monk fills it
for him.*] . . . You see, I can't make out certificates of death,
since I have no legal right any more to practice medicine, Monk.

MONK: . . . In the light of what happened, there's something
I'd better tell you, Doc. Soon as you left here to deliver that
baby, Leona ran out of the bar to make a phone call to the
office at Treasure Island, warning them that you were on your
way out there to deliver a baby. So, Doc, you may be in trouble
. . . If you stay here . . .

DOC: I'll take a Benzedrine tablet and pack and . . .

MONK: Hit the road before morning.

DOC: I'll hit the road tonight.

MONK: Don't let it hit you. [*Stands to shake.*] G'bye, Doc. Keep in touch.

DOC: G'bye, Monk. Thanks for all and the warning.

MONK: Take care, Doc.

STEVE: Yeh, Doc, you got to take care. Bye, Doc.

BILL: No sweat, Doc, g'bye.

[*Doc exits.*]

MONK: That old son of a bitch's paid his dues . . .

[*Altercation rises outside once more: "I'm gonna slap the cuffs on you! . . ." "That does it, let go of me, you fink, you pig!" Approach of a squad car siren is heard at a distance.*]

Yep, coming the law!

BILL: I don't want in on this.

STEVE: Not me neither.

[*They rush out. Squad car screeches to a stop. Leona appears at the door, shouting and pounding.*]

LEONA: MONK! THE PADDY WAGON IS SINGING MY SONG!

[*Monk lets her in and locks the door.*]

MONK: Go upstairs. Can you make it?

[*She clambers up the steps, slips, nearly falls.*

[*Policeman knocks at the door. Monk admits him.*]

Hi, Tony.

TONY: Hi, Monk. What's this about a fight going on here, Monk?

**67**

MONK: Fight? Not here. It's been very peaceful tonight. The bar is closed. I'm sitting here having a nightcap with . . .

TONY: Who's that bawling back there?

MONK: [*pouring a drink for Tony*]: Some dame disappointed in love, the usual thing. Try this and if it suits you, take the bottle.

TONY [*He drinks.*]: . . . O.K. Good.

MONK: Take the bottle. Drop in more often. I miss you.

TONY: Thanks, g'night. [*He goes out.*]

MONK: Coast is clear, Leona. [*As Monk puts another bottle on the table, Leona comes awkwardly back down the stairs.*]

LEONA: Monk? Thanks, Monk. [*She and Monk sit at the table. Violet comes out of the ladies' room.*]

VIOLET: Steve? . . . Bill? [*She sees Leona at the table and starts to retreat.*]

LEONA: Aw, hell, Violet. Come over and sit down with us, we're having a nightcap, all of us, my brother's death-day is over.

VIOLET: Why does everyone hate me? [*She sits at the table: drinks are poured from the bottle. Violet hitches her chair close to Monk's. In a few moments she will deliberately drop a matchbook under the table, bend to retrieve it, and the hand on Monk's side will not return to the table surface.*]

LEONA: Nobody hates you, Violet. It would be a compliment to you if they did.

VIOLET: I'd hate to think that I'd come between you and Bill.

LEONA: Don't torture yourself with an awful thought like that. Two people living together is something you don't understand,

and since you don't understand it you don't respect it, but, Violet, this being our last conversation, I want to advise something to you. I think you need medical help in the mental department and I think this because you remind me of a . . . of a . . . of a plant of some kind . . .

VIOLET: Because my name is Violet?

LEONA: No, I wasn't thinking of violets, I was thinking of water plants, yeah, plants that don't grow in the ground but float on water. With you everything is such a . . . such a . . . well, you know what I mean, don't you?

VIOLET: Temporary arrangement?

LEONA: Yes, you could put it that way. Do you know how you got into that place upstairs from the amusement arcade?

VIOLET: . . . How?

LEONA: Yes, *how* or *why* or *when?*

VIOLET: . . . Why, I . . . [*She obviously is uncertain on all three points.*]

LEONA: Take your time. And *think*. How, why, when?

VIOLET: Why, I was . . . in L.A., and . . .

LEONA: Are you sure you were in L.A.? Are you sure about even that? Or is everything foggy to you, is your mind in a cloud?

VIOLET: Yes, I was . . .

LEONA: I said take your time, don't push it. Can you come out of the fog?

MONK: Leona, take it easy, we all know Violet's got problems.

LEONA: Her problems are mental problems and I want her to face them, now, in our last conversation. Violet? Can you come out of the fog and tell us how, when, and why you're living out of a suitcase upstairs from the amusement arcade, can you just . . .

MONK: [*cutting in*]: She's left the amusement arcade, she left it tonight, she came here with her suitcase.

LEONA: Yeah, she's a water plant, with roots in water, drifting the way it takes her. .

[*Violet weeps.*]

And she cries too easy, the water works are back on. I'll give her some music to cry to before I go back to my home on wheels and get it cracking up the Old Spanish Trail. [*She rises from the table.*]

MONK: Not tonight, Leona. You have to sleep off your liquor before you get on the highway in this fog.

LEONA: That's what you think, not what I think, Monk. My time's run out in this place. [*She has walked to the juke box and started the violin piece.*] . . . How, when, and why, and her only answer is tears. Couldn't say how, couldn't say when, couldn't say why. And I don't think she's sure where she was before she come here, any more sure than she is where she'll go when she leaves here. She don't dare remember and she don't dare look forward, neither. Her mind floats on a cloud and her body floats on water. And her dirty fingernail hands reach out to hold onto something she hopes can hold her together. [*She starts back toward the table, stops; the bar dims and light is focused on her.*] . . . Oh, my God, she's at it again, she got a hand under the table. [*Leona laughs sadly.*] Well, I guess she can't help it. It's sad, though. It's a pitiful thing to have to reach under a table to find some reason to live. You know, she's worshipping her idea of God Almighty in her personal church. Why the hell should I care she done it to a nowhere person that I put up in my trailer for a few months?

I wish that kid from I-oh-a with eyes like my lost brother had been willing to travel with me, but I guess I scared him. What I think I'll do is turn back to a faggot's moll when I haul up to Sausalito or San Francisco. You always find one in the gay bars that needs a big sister with him, to camp with and laugh and cry with, and I hope I'll find one soon . . . it scares me to be alone in my home on wheels built for two . . . [*She turns as the bar is lighted and goes back to the table.*] Monk, HEY, MONK! What's my tab here t'night?

MONK: Forget it, don't think about it, go home and sleep, Leona. [*He and Violet appear to be in a state of trance together.*]

LEONA: I'm not going to sleep and I never leave debts behind me. This twenty ought to do it. [*She places a bill on the table.*]

MONK: Uh-huh, sure, keep in touch . . .

LEONA: Tell Bill he'll find his effects in the trailer-court office, and when he's hustled himself a new meal ticket, he'd better try and respect her, at least in public . . . . Well . . . [*She extends her hand slightly. Monk and Violet are sitting with closed eyes.*]

. . . I guess I've already gone.

VIOLET: G'bye, Leona.

MONK: G'bye . . .

LEONA: "Meglior solo," huh, ducks? [*Leona lets herself out of the bar.*]

MONK: . . . G'bye, Leona.

VIOLET: . . . Monk?

MONK: [*correctly suspecting her intent*]: You want your suitcase, it's . . .

VIOLET: I don't mean my suitcase, nothing valuable's in it but my . . . undies and . . .

MONK: Then what've you got in mind?

VIOLET: . . . In *what?*

MONK: Sorry. No offense meant. But there's taverns licensed for rooms, and taverns licensed for liquor and food and liquor, and I am a tavern only licensed for . . .

VIOLET: [*overlapping with a tone and gesture of such ultimate supplication that it would break the heart of a stone*]: I just meant . . . let's go upstairs. Huh? Monk? [*Monk stares at her reflectively for a while, considering all the potential complications of her taking up semi- or permanent residence up there.*] Why're you looking at me that way? I just want a temporary, a night, a . . .

MONK: . . . Yeah, go on up and make yourself at home. Take a shower up there while I lock up the bar.

VIOLET: God love you, Monk, like me. [*She crosses, with a touch of "labyrinthitis," to the stairs and mounts two steps.*] Monk! . . . I'm scared of these stairs, they're almost steep as a ladder. I better take off my slippers. Take my slippers off for me. [*There is a tone in her voice that implies she has already "moved in" . . . She holds out one leg from the steps, then the other. Monk removes her slippers and she goes on up, calling down to him:*] Bring up some beer, sweetheart.

MONK: Yeh, I'll bring some beer up. Don't forget your shower. [*Alone in the bar, Monk crosses downstage.*] I'm going to stay down here till I hear that shower running, I am not going up there till she's took a shower. [*He sniffs the ratty slipper.*] Dirty, worn-out slipper still being worn, sour-smelling with sweat from being worn too long, but still set by the bed to be worn again the next day, walked on here and there on—pointless—errands till the sole's worn through, and even then not thrown away, just padded with cardboard till the cardboard's worn through and still not thrown away, still put on to walk on till it's . . . past all repair . . . [*He has been, during this, turning out lamps in the bar.*] Hey, Violet, will you for Chrissake take a . . . [*This shouted appeal breaks off with a disgusted laugh. He drops the slipper, then grins sadly.*] She probably thinks she'd dissolve in water. I shouldn't of let her stay here. Well, I won't touch her, I'll have no contact with her, maybe I won't even go up there tonight. [*He crosses to open the door. We hear the boom of the ocean outside.*] I always leave the door open for a few minutes to clear the smoke and liquor smell out of the place, the human odors, and to hear the ocean. Y'know, it sounds different this late than it does with the crowd on the beach-front. It has a private sound to it, a sound that's just for itself and for me. [*Monk switches off the blue neon sign. It goes dark outside. He closes door.*]

[*Sound of water running above. He slowly looks toward the sound.*]

That ain't rain.

[*Tired from the hectic night, maybe feeling a stitch of pain in his heart (but he's used to that), Monk starts to the stairs. In the spill of light beneath them, he glances up with a slow smile, wry, but not bitter. A smile that's old too early, but it grows a bit warmer as he starts up the stairs.*]

CURTAIN

# NOTES AFTER THE SECOND
# INVITED AUDIENCE:

## (And a Troubled Sleep.)

The play has drifted out of focus: I was almost inclined to think, "My God, this is a play about groping!"

The production of this play, and I think the play itself, deserves something better than that. The designer, the lighting and sound men, have caught perfectly the mood, the poetry, the ambience of the play.

But unfortunately in performance that lyricism—which is, as always, what I must chiefly rely upon as a playwright—is not being fully explored and utilized. At this moment, I must make a number of exceptions which will be made privately: I would say, however, to all the cast that at last night's performance the only parts that were totally and beautifully realized were those of "Doc," "Steve," "Quentin," and "Bobby."

We have now arrived at a point where we must approach this undertaking with the same seriousness—and I do not mean ponderousness but the opposite of ponderousness—that I had buried somewhere in me, beneath the liquor and the drugs that made my life a death-time in the late sixties; a sort of lyric appeal to my remnant of life to somehow redeem and save me —not from life's end, which can't be revealed through any court of appeals, but from a sinking into shadow and eclipse of so much of everything that had made my life meaningful to me.

I am sorry to return to a self-concerned note. Believe me, my concern is now much broader than self-concern, and in this particular instance, the case of this play and its players and its producers and its artists—which all of you certainly are (I doubt that you can believe how much I care for each of you as a person, and with the truest and purest kind of caring)—I would set down as an axiom that a playwright should never direct his work unassisted by someone who shares his concept but is better able to implement it through discipline.

The word "discipline" is not a pretty word to bring up at this point, and yet it must be. I am too old a hand at the abuse of self-discipline to fail to recognize a failure of self-discipline when I see it so nakedly on a stage before audiences.

The clinical name for this failure to discipline the self to achieve its goal is "the impulse toward self-destruction," which is the opposite and dark side of the will to create and to flower.

Self-transcendence, as well as self-discipline, is now in order. Each of us must put aside as best we can his and her personal stake in this adventure, this play, in order to serve its true creation as a whole. Ensemble and entity must take precedence, now, over that Mae West line to her manager, "How did the lady come on tonight?"—the wonderful bitch did not expect to receive a negative response, and she never got one, but it's a pity he didn't catch her act in the "Breckinridge" comeback. Or speak up about it.

Now to specifics about *Small Craft Warnings:*

I know that our designer, Fred Voelpel, will move that sailfish about a foot and a half out from the wall of the bar and have it suspended over the bar directly, with always just a bit of a light on its astonished expression. This will not upstage but will just provide a muted but persistent key to the tender irony which is the keynote to the still-possible success of this play.

Right now what troubles me most—in the way of specific staging and writing—is that, as physical climaxes to both acts, we have such closely corresponding chase-scenes of Violet by Leona. Of course this could be solved by returning to the opening of *Confessional** and starting the play with Violet wailing in the ladies' room and Leona pacing about in the middle of a

* Included in *Dragon Country* (New Directions, New York, 1970).

tirade. This would eliminate one chase scene. However, it would also eliminate the establishment of place, situation, and identification of characters. And, incidentally, it would finally persuade me that I am no longer able to write a Goddam thing for the American theatre.

The other option—which I hope we can take—is to sharply differentiate the second chase scene from the first. I love the return of Steve and Bill, but I don't like the total absence of a "rhubarb" on the beach until the squad car siren is heard. I think something better than this can somehow be managed for us. I think that Leona has been in furious altercation with a cop or watchman on the beach-front all this time, and the sound of it should "bleed under" like the lights "bleed under" Doc's big monologue. But let us be aware it is going on out there, although —for the uses of a really not literal or naturalistic play—it is faded under the monologue till that has scored for us and is then brought up again a few beats preceding Leona's rush back into the bar, because the beach cop has finally had to call the wagon for her.

For a while, let Leona ad-lib the altercation outside at a level set by the director—and meanwhile, I will write it. Let's say, for the moment, it goes something like this:

LEONA: Okay, do that! I just dare you to do that! Call the wagon! I'm willing to ride in a wagon! It's got wheels, I'll ride in any Goddam thing on wheels, I'm just the one to do it! Okay? Want to call the wagon out here for me? What are you waiting for? Me to go? Oh, no, I'm not going yet. Take your hand off my arm, you fuckin' pig! Don't put your hand on the arm of a lady! [*Sound of a slap: then Bill rushes back in to make his phone call.*]

I think that there can be an interior of bar "hold" for this loud outside altercation between Leona and the beach cop right after Monk calls Doc over to the table: he can do this before

Bill and Steve enter. And there can be a dramatic tension in Doc's unreadiness to tell of the disasters at Treasure Island for the time that Leona's off-stage rhubarb with the beach cop is heard. At the end of the Doc's story and just after his exit, Leona's voice can be heard again, continuing her rhubarb with the beach cop: "All right, I'm waiting, I am standing here waiting till that wagon gets here"—then the siren begins:

> LEONA: That does it, let go of me, you fink, you pig!" [*Having struggled free of the beach cop's clasp on her arm, she now charges back into the bar, crying out:*] MONK! THE PADDY-WAGON IS SINGING MY SONG!

And let us please have "singing," not "playing."
Other specifics:
I think I've already gotten across to you the necessity of building up those elements in the play not concerned with the groin and the groping so that the audiences will recognize that this is not a sordid piece of writing. Now I think—with the exception of "Steve"—everybody in the cast—except "Monk" and "Doc"—is giving us a Bowery drunk bit, and that's not where the play's at. We don't want to sit out there looking at "vulnerable human vessels" that can touch us with their individual hearts, each at a time of crisis that compels it to cry out.

Finally, unless there's a sudden upsurge of energies and of selective focus, I think we need a later opening than is now scheduled.* I have always opposed an Easter Sunday opening for very personal but understandable reasons. Now I oppose it for reasons that seem almost desperately practical. The play strikes me as inviting disaster unless it is given time to pull itself together from its present state—and I gravely doubt that four more days are enough. It seems to me that the book has to be studied till there is no longer any groping after lines. Till mugging is not substituted for the delivery of the right ones.

* Sunday, April 2, 1972.

**77**

I have always suspected that actors regard playwrights as hostile beings, and this has always made me shy around them. I hope you prove me wrong, since we are all sitting together in this small craft and have been warned by two audiences that the sea is very rough.

However, at this moment I prefer the *Marseillaise* to "extreme unction."

*Corággio!*

T. W.

## SMALL CRAFT WARNINGS:
## GENESIS AND EVOLUTION

A well-received production in the summer of 1971 at Bar Harbor, Maine, of Tennessee Williams's *Confessional* prompted him to expand and reshape this earlier short play into the longer work, *Small Craft Warnings*. The following excerpts are selected from the playwright's correspondence with Bill Barnes (his agent), William Hunt (who was responsible for the Maine performances), and Robert Currie, Mario De Maria, and William Orton (the producers of *Small Craft Warnings*).

Key West, October 17, 1971

Dear Bill:

I'm writing you on my secretary's self-designed stationary. He's making a similar batch for me with my name in smaller type and without the cabalistic inscriptions on the left margin.

I am enclosing a revised draft of the curtain-raiser of *Two Plays*, the project for off-Broadway this season. Would you please get it typed up for me. . . .

It reads slow but I feel it would play well and that the end would be touching, and it seems very "now."

When I come back up in early December for Dotson's benefit thing at the Episcopal Cathedral, could a reading of the two plays be arranged for possible backers? With gifted actors reading? I feel it's so important, psychologically, for me to stay active in the theatre and just staying active is sufficient for my purposes, I don't need more than the assurance that I am not prematurely counted out as an active playwright. —Like swimming and love, it's all that keeps me going.

Yours fondly,
10.
Tenn.

P.S. The above *cri de coeur* is obsoleted by our phone talk and the news about *Confessional*. I have read that one over: it is all well written, I think, the main problem being too much writing. But a truly good production could bring it to life so sharply that the overwriting would be generally excused, if anything I do is still excused by the press. . . .

Key West, October 25, 1971

Dear Mr. Hunt:

My new agent, Bill Barnes at IFA, called me a couple of nights ago to say that you were interested in an off-Broadway production of *Confessional*—which I hope is true. It's very important to me to stay active in the theatre, I only feel half alive when I'm not.

I recall receiving from you last summer in Chicago some photos and résumés of actors for a Maine production of this play but the Chicago situation was so frantic that I could give no attention to anything else. I would certainly be interested in knowing how the production worked out. It's a very demanding play with all of those long "arias" and the heavy content: but when I read it over, the writing seemed good and some of the characters, notably "Violet" and "Leona," struck me as quite touching and funny. In any case, it might prove an interesting enterprise for off-Broadway this season.

Would you let me hear from you about it? I am taking an apartment in New Orleans for two or three months but do not yet have an address there. I will be here in Key West till this coming Sunday. After that I'll be briefly at the Hotel Royal Orleans while apartment-hunting and for a week end in Houston to see the Alley Theatre production of *Camino Real*. If you feel like traveling, I would be happy to have you as a guest in the New Orleans apartment when I have one, or we might even get together at the Houston gig. . . .

> With due apologies, cordially,
> Tennessee


New Orleans, November 1, 1971

Dear Bill Hunt:

Many thanks for sending me the notices. They are about the best I've received in ten years and clearly indicate that you did an excellent job on the play. The promise of some action in the New York theatre gives me a much-needed boost of morale. . . . I would gather from the notices that the play was well and carefully cast in Maine. Perhaps my favorite part in *Confessional* is that of "Violet". . . .

It is possible that I will get to New York late this month as Barnes wants me to tape a TV interview there: that would give us a chance to meet personally and discuss all aspects of the project and get it moving.

Barnes feels that the second scene of the play is too short: which may be, but it strikes me as the most natural point of division. I am not satisfied with the final bit, "Monk's" monologue about the slipper. I like the speech but it seems to give the play an unnecessarily bleak curtain. I wondered if he could not cross to the open door and stand there inhaling the ocean air deeply for the curtain: the waves booming as the set disappears in mist. Sometimes a bit of business like that can offer a sort of catharsis without words.

If I am not able to get to New York, it would be great if you could visit me here in New Orleans. I am taking an apartment tomorrow which is said to have an attractive guest room. (No good—still looking.)

It is four a.m. and I am tired after my flight from Key West: but happy over the way things are shaping up.

With warmest regards,
Tennessee

New Orleans, December 13, 1971

Dear Billy:

. . . I have no intentions of not participating in the making of this production. As I said . . . last night, "You know that I am going to be reviewed more than the play and that is how it has been for the last ten years." It is wrong and a scandal but that is how it has been and will be, perhaps more than ever. I want each one of those male roles to be cast as well as they can possibly be cast: THE PLAY NEEDS IT." —So far, in the male roles I am totally satisfied only with "The Boy." I think we can get superior actors for all the other men in the play. Since this play is so much talk and character, stock players, even if the best stock players, will not suffice. . . .

Please don't fear that I am going to come on like gang-busters. I am a reticent man. But I have too much at stake in the show—morally, I mean. . . . We can and we gotta get better!

Right on! With love,
10.

New Orleans, December 21, 1971

Dear Bill:

Here is a batch of rewrites in varying degrees of completion. You all will notice that my intent is to focus the play more on Helena. And to provide more action, to balance the monologues. I have also suggested an alternative title.

. . . I feel very fortunate to have these three young producers and I do not want to jeopardize the production by extended contract negotiations. I think the producers' contract—unless it demands my immediate decapitation—ought to be signed at once so they can move. . . .

I am not into money-making gimmicks but artistic advantages. I think Bill, Bob, and Mario will assure them for us. The size of the cast is formidable: the actors have to be fine ones:—everything possible should be done to enhance the play's chance of production and survival, I mean from the producers' and backers' POV . . .

So much for business. . . .

Yours,
10.

New Orleans, January 1, 1972

Dear Bill:

By the end of this week we'll be in Key West where I'll stay in our other *pied-á-terre* till I hear from you. It's turned cold here, I need a couple of week's sun to prepare me for what I *still* hope will bring me back to New York. . . .

But I'm not a man who can live on prospects continually deferred. You know, one side of the three—or is it four?—

dimensional continuum that we live in is that relentless thing called time, and I feel it running out on me, so when things remain in a state of nebulous prospects, well, my feet get itchy. Isn't it plausible to suppose that if the off-Broadway gig was really going to occur, if the money was really there, wouldn't there be a house set for it by this time, and wouldn't "the full steam ahead" be a palpable if not visual force? . . .

Please let me know what progress or regression or total collapse has occurred before I leave here this week end: I've got to know to make plans.

With warmest regards,
Tennessee

Key West, January 20, 1971

Dear Bill:

I get strong vibes over the phone and I sensed that nobody wants me to change a thing in the play. OK, I won't. But just let it end with the transposition, "Monk," at the open door, letting the human odors out of the place and breathing the ocean.

I feel about this play that it can't do any harm, even if it fails to do good to anyone but Helena. And since I love that girl, I will settle for that. . . .

After some reflection—I think "The Truck & Warehouse Theatre"* has a lovely sound to it. Could it be interpreted as a metaphor for posterity . . .

With affection,
Tennessee

---

* *Small Craft Warnings* opened at The Truck and Warehouse Theatre in New York on April 2, 1972.

**84**

New York, April 24, 1972

Dear Mario, Bob, and Bill:

Knowing from long experience that the sight of the play-wright is temporarily odious to actors and producers of a play in trouble, I have had the discretion to stay away from the scene of my (probably) last New York production.

However I want to repeat that I've never had producers with whom it was happier for me to work, nor a cast . . . that I felt more affection toward. . . .

I am delivering to Billy Barnes today some last rewrites—one which I think might be particularly helpful: a dialogue between "Doc" and "Monk" which—with good timing and style of delivery—would keep the stage alive during the off-stage bru-haha which isn't or wasn't quite happening the last time I saw the show.

Please read it over a couple of times before you dismiss it. It makes of those stairs to the living quarter above a very organic thing.

Thank you for a very lovely production.

Fondest best wishes to all,
Tennessee

Lafayette (Indiana), April 27, 1972

Dear Mario: Bill: Bob:

There are several things besides my return to New York and further saturation interviews and talk-shows that can be done to improve the situation at the T. & W.

I know it's no use suggesting that the show be transferred to a theatre further uptown or in a section less associated in the public mind with the hazards of the ghetto. The set could probably not be fitted onto another off-B'dway stage.

The gig which I completed here last night was something for the books. We had to play to a banquet hall with two wings— it reminded me of the old Penn Station in N. Y. Still, it held. And we got a standing ovation.

I leave this afternoon for Minneapolis (University of Minnesota) where I shall do my fan dance with falling feathers and a kangaroo partner. So life goes on and on when your heart belongs to show biz.

With love as ever,
10.

Key West, May 10, 1972

Dear Bill:

When I get a really good night's sleep I usually hit a good day at work. I am sending you a really good piece of writing for the top of SCW. Of course I don't know if it is still running but if it is, this new beginning could really send it off to a good start. Why don't we let it be known that the play is still being worked on and improved so that there will be fresh interest in it? . . .

I hope you will see why I am characterizing and building up "Doc" so much. He has to be a major character, full dimension, at the end of the play.*

Love,
Tenn.

---

* Tennessee Williams made his acting debut on June 6, 1972, playing the role of "Doc" for the first five performances at The New Theatre, in New York, where the production had relocated.

# Some New Directions Paperbooks

Walter Abish, *Alphabetical Africa*. NDP375.
*In the Future Perfect*. NDP440.
*Minds Meet*. NDP387.
Illangô Adigal, *Shilappadikaram*. NDP162.
Alain, *The Gods*. NDP382
Wayne Andrews. *Voltaire*. NDP519.
David Antin, *Talking at the Boundaries*. NDP388.
G. Apollinaire, *Selected Writings*.† NDP310.
Djuna Barnes, *Nightwood*. NDP98.
Charles Baudelaire, *Flowers of Evil*.† NDP71,
*Paris Spleen*. NDP294.
Martin Bax, *The Hospital Ship*. NDP402.
Gottfried Benn, *Primal Vision*.† NDP322.
Wolfgang Borchert, *The Man Outside*. NDP319.
Jorge Luis Borges, *Labyrinths*. NDP186.
Jean-Francois Bory, *Once Again* NDP256.
E. Brock, *Here. Now. Always*. NDP429.
*The Portraits & The Poses*. NDP360.
*The River and the Train*. NDP478.
Buddha, *The Dhammapada*. NDP188.
Frederick Busch, *Domestic Particulars*. NDP413.
*Manual Labor*. NDP376.
Ernesto Cardenal, *Apocalypse*. NDP441. *In Cuba*.
NDP377. *Zero Hour*. NDP502.
Hayden Carruth, *For You*. NDP298.
*From Snow and Rock, from Chaos*. NDP349.
Louis-Ferdinand Céline,
*Death on the Installment Plan* NDP330.
*Journey to the End of the Night*. NDP84.
Jean Cocteau, *The Holy Terrors*. NDP212.
*The Infernal Machine*. NDP235.
M. Cohen, *Monday Rhetoric*. NDP352.
Robert Coles, *Irony in the Mind's Life*. NDP459.
Cid Corman, *Livingdying*. NDP289.
*Sun Rock Man*. NDP318.
Gregory Corso, *Elegiac Feelings*. NDP299.
*Happy Birthday of Death*. NDP86.
*Long Live Man*. NDP127.
Robert Creeley, *Hello*. NDP451.
*Later*. NDP488.
Edward Dahlberg, *Reader*. NDP246.
*Because I Was Flesh*. NDP227.
Osamu Dazai, *The Setting Sun*. NDP258.
*No Longer Human*. NDP357.
Coleman Dowell, *Mrs. October . . .* NDP368.
*Too Much Flesh and Jabez*. NDP447.
Robert Duncan, *Bending the Bow*. NDP255.
*The Opening of the Field*. NDP356.
*Roots and Branches*. NDP275.
Dutch "Fiftiers," *Living Space*. NDP493.
Richard Eberhart, *Selected Poems*. NDP198.
E. F. Edinger, *Melville's Moby-Dick*. NDP460.
Russell Edson, *The Falling Sickness*. NDP389.
Wm. Empson, *7 Types of Ambiguity*. NDP204.
*Some Versions of Pastoral*. NDP92.
Wm. Everson, *Man-Fate*, NDP369.
*The Residual Years*. NDP263.
Lawrence Ferlinghetti, *Her*. NDP88.
*A Coney Island of the Mind*. NDP74.
*Endless Life*. NDP516.
*The Mexican Night*. NDP300.
*The Secret Meaning of Things*. NDP268.
*Starting from San Francisco*. NDP220.
*Tyrannus Nix?*. NDP288.
*Unfair Arguments . . .* NDP143
*Who Are We Now?* NDP425.
Ronald Firbank. *Five Novels*. NDP518.
F. Scott Fitzgerald, *The Crack-up*. NDP54.
Robert Fitzgerald, *Spring Shade*. NDP311.
Gustave Flaubert, *Dictionary*. NDP230.
Gandhi, *Gandhi on Non-Violence*. NDP197.
Goethe, *Faust*, Part I. NDP70.
Henry Green. *Back*. NDP517.
Allen Grossman, *The Woman on the Bridge*
*Over the Chicago River*. NDP473.
John Hawkes, *The Beetle Leg*. NDP239.
*The Blood Oranges*. NDP338.
*The Cannibal*. NDP123.
*Death Sleep & The Traveler*. NDP393.
*The Innocent Party*. NDP238.
*The Lime Twig*. NDP95.
*The Owl*. NDP443.

*Second Skin*. NDP146.
*Travesty*. NDP430.
A. Hayes, *A Wreath of Christmas Poems*.
NDP347.
Samuel Hazo. *To Paris*. NDP512.
H. D., *End to Torment*. NDP476.
*Helen in Egypt*. NDP380.
*Hermetic Definition*. NDP343.
*Trilogy*. NDP362.
Robert E. Helbling, *Heinrich von Kleist*, NDP390.
Hermann Hesse, *Siddhartha*. NDP65.
C. Isherwood, *All the Conspirators*. NDP480.
*The Berlin Stories*. NDP134.
Philippe Jaccottet, *Seedtime*. NDP428.
Alfred Jarry, *The Supermale*. NDP426.
*Ubu Roi*. NDP105.
Robinson Jeffers, *Cawdor and Media*. NDP293.
James Joyce, *Stephen Hero*. NDP133.
*James Joyce/Finnegans Wake*. NDP331.
Franz Kafka, *Amerika*. NDP117.
Bob Kaufman,
*The Ancient Rain*. NDP514.
*Solitudes Crowded with Loneliness*. NDP199.
Hugh Kenner, *Wyndham Lewis*. NDP167.
Kenyon Critics, *G. M. Hopkins*. NDP355.
H. von Kleist, *Prince Friedrich of Homburg*.
NDP462.
Elaine Kraf, *The Princess of 72nd St*. NDP494.
P. Lal, *Great Sanskrit Plays*. NDP142.
Lautréamont, *Maldoror*. NDP207.
Irving Layton, *Selected Poems*. NDP431.
Denise Levertov, *Collected Earlier*. NDP475.
*Footprints*. NDP344.
*The Freeing of the Dust*. NDP401.
*The Jacob's Ladder*. NDP112.
*Life in the Forest*. NDP461.
*The Poet in the World*. NDP363.
*Relearning the Alphabet*. NDP290.
*The Sorrow Dance*. NDP222.
*To Stay Alive*. NDP325.
Harry Levin, *James Joyce*. NDP87.
Li Ch'ing-chao, *Complete Poems*. NDP492.
Enrique Lihn, *The Dark Room*.† NDP452.
García Lorca, *The Cricket Sings*.† NDP506.
*Deep Song*. NDP503.
*Five Plays*. NDP232.
*Selected Poems*.† NDP114.
*Three Tragedies*. NDP52.
Michael McClure, *Gorf*. NDP416.
*Antechamber*. NDP455.
*Jaguar Skies*. NDP400.
*Josephine: The Mouse Singer*. NDP496.
Carson McCullers, *The Member of the*
*Wedding*. (Playscript) NDP153.
Thomas Merton, *Asian Journal*. NDP394.
*Collected Poems*. NDP504.
*Gandhi on Non-Violence*. NDP197.
*News Seeds of Contemplation*. NDP337.
*Raids on the Unspeakable*. NDP213.
*Selected Poems*. NDP85.
*The Way of Chuang Tzu*. NDP276.
*The Wisdom of the Desert*. NDP295.
*Zen and the Birds of Appetite*. NDP261.
Henry Miller, *The Air-Conditioned Nightmare*.
NDP302.
*Big Sur & The Oranges*. NDP161.
*The Books in My Life*. NDP280.
*The Colossus of Maroussi*. NDP75.
*The Cosmological Eye*. NDP109.
*Henry Miller on Writing*. NDP151.
*The Henry Miller Reader*. NDP269.
*Just Wild About Harry*. NDP479.
*The Smile at the Foot of the Ladder*. NDP386.
*Stand Still Like the Hummingbird*. NDP236.
*The Time of the Assassins*. NDP115.
Y. Mishima, *Confessions of a Mask*. NDP253.
*Death in Midsummer*. NDP215.
Eugenio Montale, *It Depends*.† NDP507.
*New Poems*. NDP410.
*Selected Poems*.† NDP193.
Vladimir Nabokov, *Nikolai Gogol*. NDP78.
*Laughter in the Dark*. NDP470.
*The Real Life of Sebastian Knight*. NDP432.
P. Neruda, *The Captain's Verses*.† NDP345.
*Residence on Earth*.† NDP340.

*New Directions in Prose & Poetry* (Anthology).
  Available from #17 forward. #42, Fall 1981.
Robert Nichols, *Arrival.* NDP437.
  *Exile.* NDP485. *Garh City.* NDP450.
  *Harditts in Sawna.* NDP470.
Charles Olson. *Selected Writings.* NDP231.
Toby Olson, *The Life of Jesus.* NDP417.
George Oppen, *Collected Poems.* NDP418.
Wilfred Owen, *Collected Peoms.* NDP210.
Nicanor Parra, *Emergency Poems.*† NDP333.
  *Poems and Antipoems.*† NDP242.
Boris Pasternak, *Safe Conduct.* NDP77.
Kenneth Patchen. *Aflame and Afun.* NDP292.
  *Because It Is.* NDP83.
  *But Even So.* NDP265.
  *Collected Poems.* NDP284.
  *Doubleheader.* NDP211.
  *Hallelujah Anyway.* NDP219.
  *In Quest of Candlelighters.* NDP334.
  *Memoirs of a Shy Pornographer.* NDP205.
  *Selected Poems.* NDP160.
Octavio Paz, *Configurations.*† NDP303.
  *A Draft of Shadows.*† NDP489.
  *Eagle or Sun?*† NDP422.
  *Early Poems.*† NDP354.
*Plays for a New Theater.* (Anth.) NDP216.
J. A. Porter, *Eelgrass.* NDP438.
Ezra Pound, *ABC of Reading.* NDP89.
  *Classic Noh Theatre of Japan.* NDP79.
  *Confucius.* NDP285.
  *Confucius to Cummings.* (Anth.) NDP126.
  *Gaudier Brzeska.* NDP372.
  *Guide to Kulchur.* NDP257.
  *Literary Essays.* NDP250.
  *Love Poems of Ancient Egypt.* NDP178.
  *Pound/Joyce.* NDP296.
  *Selected Cantos.* NDP304.
  *Selected Letters 1907-1941.* NDP317.
  *Selected Poems.* NDP66.
  *The Spirit of Romance.* NDP266.
  *Translations.*† (Enlarged Edition) NDP145.
James Purdy, *Children Is All.* NDP327.
Raymond Queneau, *The Bark Tree.* NDP314.
  *Exercises in Style.* NDP513.
  *The Sunday of Life.* NDP433.
  *We Always Treat Women Too Well.* NDP515.
Mary de Rachewiltz, *Ezra Pound.* NDP405.
M. Randall, *Part of the Solution.* NDP350.
John Crowe Ransom, *Beating the Bushes.*
  NDP324.
Raja Rao, *Kanthapura.* NDP224.
Herbert Read, *The Green Child.* NDP208.
P. Reverdy, *Selected Poems.*† NDP346.
Kenneth Rexroth, *Collected Longer Poems.*
  NDP309.
  *Collected Shorter Poems.* NDP243.
  *The Morning Star.* NDP490.
  *New Poems.* NDP383.
  *100 More Poems from the Chinese.* NDP308.
  *100 More Poems from the Japanese.* NDP420.
  *100 Poems from the Chinese.* NDP192.
  *100 Poems from the Japanese.*† NDP147.
Rainer Maria Rilke, *Poems from*
  *The Book of Hours.* NDP408.
  *Possibility of Being.* (Poems). NDP436.
  *Where Silence Reigns.* (Prose). NDP464.
Arthur Rimbaud, *Illuminations.*† NDP56.
  *Season in Hell & Drunken Boat.*† NDP97.
Edouard Roditi, *Delights of Turkey.* NDP445.
Selden Rodman, *Tongues of Fallen Angels.*
  NDP373.
Jerome Rothenberg, *Poland/1931.* NDP379.
  *Pre-Faces.* NDP511.
  *Seneca Journal.* NDP448.
  *Vienna Blood.* NDP498.
Saigyo,† *Mirror for the Moon.* NDP465.
Saikaku Ihara. *The Life of an Amorous*
  *Woman.* NDP270.
St. John of the Cross, *Poems.*† NDP341.
Jean-Paul Sartre, *Baudelaire.* NDP233.

*Nausea.* NDP82.
  *The Wall (Intimacy).* NDP272.
Delmore Schwartz, *Selected Poems.* NDP241.
  *In Dreams Begin Responsibilities.* NDP454.
Kazuko Shiraishi, *Seaons of Sacred Lust.*
  NDP453.
Stevie Smith, *Selected Poems,* NDP159.
Gary Snyder, *The Back Country.* NDP249.
  *Earth House Hold.* NDP267.
  *Myths and Texts.* NDP457.
  *The Real Work.* NDP499.
  *Regarding Wave.* NDP306.
  *Turtle Island.* NDP381.
Enid Starkie, *Rimbaud.* NDP254.
Robert Steiner, *Bathers.* NDP495
Stendhal, *The Telegraph.* NDP108.
Jules Supervielle, *Selected Writings.*† NDP209.
W. Sutton, *American Free Verse.* NDP351.
Nathaniel Tarn, *Lyrics . . . Bride of God.* NDP391.
Dylan Thomas, *Adventures in the Skin Trade.*
  NDP183.
  *A Child's Christmas in Wales.* NDP181.
  *Collected Poems 1934-1952.* NDP316.
  *The Doctor and the Devils.* NDP297.
  *Portrait of the Artist as a Young Dog.*
  NDP51.
  *Quite Early One Morning.* NDP90.
  *Under Milk Wood.* NDP73.
Lionel Trilling. *E. M. Forster.* NDP189.
Martin Turnell. *Art of French Fiction.* NDP251.
  *Baudelaire.* NDP336.
  *Rise of the French Novel.* NDP474.
Paul Valéry, *Selected Writings.*† NDP184.
P. Van Ostaijen, *Feasts of Fear & Agony.*
  NDP411.
Elio Vittorini, *A Vittorini Omnibus.* NDP366.
  *Women of Messina.* NDP365.
Vernon Watkins, *Selected Poems.* NDP221.
Nathanael West, *Miss Lonelyhearts &*
  *Day of the Locust.* NDP125.
J. Williams, *An Ear in Bartram's Tree.* NDP335.
Tennessee Williams, *Camino Real,* NDP301.
  *Cat on a Hot Tin Roof.* NDP398.
  *Dragon Country.* NDP287.
  *The Glass Menagerie.* NDP218.
  *Hard Candy.* NDP225.
  *In the Winter of Cities.* NDP154.
  *A Lovely Sunday for Creve Coeur.* NDP497.
  *One Arm & Other Stories.* NDP237.
  *A Streetcar Named Desire.* NDP501.
  *Sweet Bird of Youth.* NDP409.
  *Twenty-Seven Wagons Full of Cotton.* NDP217.
  *Two-Character Play.* NDP483.
  *Vieux Carré.* NDP482.
  *Where I Live.* NDP468.
William Carlos Williams.
  *The Autobiography.* NDP223.
  *The Build-up.* NDP223.
  *The Farmers' Daughters.* NDP106.
  *I Wanted to Write a Poem.* NDP469.
  *Imaginations.* NDP329.
  *In the American Grain.* NDP53.
  *In the Money.* NDP240.
  *Many Loves.* NDP191.
  *Paterson.* Complete. NDP152.
  *Pictures form Brueghel.* NDP118.
  *The Selected Essays.* NDP273.
  *Selected Poems.* NDP131.
  *A Voyage to Pagany.* NDP307.
  *White Mule.* NDP226.
  *W. C. Williams Reader.* NDP282.
Yvor Winters, *E. A. Robinson.* NDP326.
Wisdom Books: *Ancient Egyptians,* NDP467.
  *Early Buddhists,* NDP444; *English Mystics,*
  NDP466; *Forest* (Hindu), NDP414; *Jewish*
  *Mystics,* NDP423; *Spanish Mystics,* NDP442;
  *St. Francis,* NDP477; *Sufi,* NDP424; *Taoists,*
  NDP509; *Wisdom of the Desert,* NDP295; *Zen*
  *Masters,* NDP415.

For complete listing request complete catalog from
New Directions, 80 Eighth Avenue, New York 10011

† Bilingual